AF473833

THE PONT-AVEN SCHOOL

CRADLE OF THE MODERN SENSIBILITY

THE PONT-AVEN SCHOOL

CRADLE OF THE MODERN SENSIBILITY

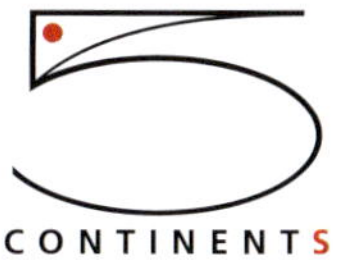

5 CONTINENTS EDITIONS

Editorial Coordination
Laura Maggioni

Art Direction
Annarita De Sanctis

Translations
Julian Comoy

Editing
Emily Ligniti

Colour Separation
Pixel Studio, Bresso, Italy

Alexandre Mouradian wishes to thank
for their precious help:

Alain Bénard, expert
Jacques Blazy, expert
Marion Boyer, restorer
Caroline de Courbeville, RG Les Cadres Gault
Sibille Gempp, restorer
Brigitte de Roquemaurel

Cover
Émile Bernard (1868–1941)
Portrait of Madame Schuffenecker
(Louise Lançon), 1888
Signed and dated on lower left
Oil on canvas
66 x 54 cm

ISBN: 978-88-7439-817-1

5 Continents Editions
Piazza Caiazzo, 1
20124 Milan, Italy
www.fivecontinentseditions.com

Distributed in the United States and Canada
by Harry N. Abrams, Inc., New York.
Distributed outside the United States
and Canada, excluding Italy, by Yale University
Press, London

Printed in Italy in January 2018 by Tecnostampa
- Pigini Group Printing Division, Loreto – Trevi,
Italy for 5 Continents Editions, Milan

TABLE OF CONTENTS

Paul Gauguin | Émile Bernard. A Meeting of Minds in Pont-Aven

JEAN-MARIE ROUART
ACADÉMIE FRANÇAISE

6

A Collection of Talismans. Exploring the Works Collected by Alexandre Mouradian

ADRIEN GOETZ
ACADÉMIE DES BEAUX-ARTS

8

Catalogue

ESTELLE GUILLE DES BUTTES
DIRECTOR AND CHIEF CURATOR MUSÉE DE PONT-AVEN

21

Bibliography

73

Contributors' Biographies

75

PAUL GAUGUIN | ÉMILE BERNARD
A MEETING OF MINDS IN PONT-AVEN

JEAN-MARIE ROUART, ACADÉMIE FRANÇAISE

No one has managed to fathom the mystery of some places. Endowed with a special kind of magic, they irresistibly attract genius, talent, and art. What kind of spell was it that bound painters to Pont Aven, a little village in Brittany with narrow, stony lanes, a vaguely medieval atmosphere, a lock, and Romanesque churches? Attempts have been made to account for it as stemming from the hospitality of its inhabitants, particularly those providing accommodation—the Julia inn and the Auberge Gloanec—who welcomed the artists and granted them infinite credit, or from the good-natured maids who brought a little kindness into the lives of those friendless figures. This, however, underestimates the impact of a key component of this pious village full of stoups: the work of the devil.

A devil with a seductive, poisonous genius: Gauguin. Without him, Pont-Aven may perhaps have welcomed some painters, but it wouldn't have been the hub of burgeoning talents straining to give Impressionism that fresh impetus we know.

It was Gauguin who lit a fire under this sleepy landscape, snug in its customs and beliefs, slumbering gently on the banks of its river, the Aven, and prudently sheltered from the ocean's storms. Plagued by a gnawing restlessness, unable to live with himself, often insufferable to his friends but endowed with a seductive charm, he was a natural-born hell-raiser. His instinct was to arouse, subvert, destabilize, get pulses racing. At his touch everything was galvanized. The academicism that was just one of the forms taken by the conventional mindset cracked open like an old plaster cast and what emerged was a set of new principles that had lain dormant beneath the rigid casing.

Of course, Gauguin was not alone, even though he made a greater splash by himself than all the others put together. He drew people to him like a lover. His most intense bittersweet relationship was with Émile Bernard, his associate and rival. Having already met figures who were soon to be recognized as major painters, such as Van Gogh, Toulouse-Lautrec, and Cézanne, Gauguin found that only Émile Bernard was able to go toe to toe with him. Orbiting around them were the gentle Maurice Denis, with his Franciscan sensibility, Sérusier, Seguin, and Moret, who enthusiastically helped edge Impressionism beyond its boundaries. Their discussions and quarrels were nothing if not fruitful. But it took the stimulus of the "holy buccaneer," as Degas, the first to recognize his genius, called him, to unleash the talent of these artists, to whom should be added Meijer de Haan, Maufra, and Verkade. The experience changed him, too, because this was where he gathered the raw material for his later experiments in the Pacific, revitalized by his contact with tribal art.

Thus it was that Pont-Aven, thanks to a revolution in painting, achieved legendary status and attained the kind of glory that only places that have felt the breath of destiny can boast—far more than Barbizon, another village that was home to a talented group of artists, who focused on the gentleness and tranquillity associated with the peaceful Millet and the placid Corot. The scenes depicted exude an atmosphere of muted charm. They have not been singed like Pont-Aven by the fire of unrestrained genius.

It's easy to see how this artistic and human adventure of the first order captivated Alexandre Mouradian, the great collector and founder of the Spinoza Foundation. His unerring taste led him to acquire superb works by Émile Bernard, the inventor of Synthetism—foremost of which is the wonderful portrait of Madame Schuffenecker—Maufra, Moret, and Maurice Denis, among others, thus encapsulating one of the key moments in the history of painting. Thanks to Alexandre Mouradian all the painters who worked, suffered, loved, and dreamt of glory on the banks of the Aven have been reunited in the Musée des Beaux-Arts de Pont-Aven with the places they knew so well and which they continue to haunt through their legend.

A COLLECTION OF TALISMANS

EXPLORING THE WORKS COLLECTED BY ALEXANDRE MOURADIAN

ADRIEN GOETZ, ACADÉMIE DES BEAUX-ARTS

A collection of artworks of the Pont-Aven School is always a collection of talismans. For the art lover who owns them and decides to put them on display, it's a self-portrait consisting of works assembled in a certain order. Whenever Pont-Aven is involved, one can be sure that a collection of paintings or engravings is inevitably the outcome of deliberate contemplation, of a long-pondered love for this stretch of land swept by the sea breeze, where artists who came from far and wide built a self-contained world, whose beauty and contradictions are revealed in a few pieces gathered together.

In the first place, there is a contradiction in the very name,[1] since there was never a Pont-Aven School as such, any more than there was one in Barbizon in the 1850s. There was no master looking after his brood of pupils in Pont-Aven at the time of Robert Wylie and the first American artists, as there wasn't later, at the time of Gauguin and Sérusier, nor even at the time of the later generation, in around 1900. No one ever thought of setting up a Giverny School in the village swarming with artists—from which Monet, ensconced in his house, cherished garden and studio, tried to set himself apart by immersing himself in his work—perhaps because Monet did his very utmost to avoid playing the part of *chef d'école*, surrounded by followers he had never chosen.

Pont-Aven is a perfectly real village, of course, but it's above all an *arrière-pays*, in the sense Yves Bonnefoy used this word, which can be loosely rendered as "hinterland," to give a label to his ruminations on "background landscapes" in Piero della Francesca's paintings—magical places that exist only in artists' imaginations, where "the visible and the close-at-hand blend."[2]

This hinterland of the soul and mind, impregnated with the salty wind and sea spray of the nearby cliffs, is a world apart, a land's end, an inner Finistère where artists could cast off their shackles. Each painting they took away with them turned into a kind of lucky charm—for themselves, for the collectors who love them, and for the museums who exhibit them. Alexandre Mouradian is well aware of this, when he expresses his admiration for Émile Bernard, who in 1888, at the age of twenty, invented a new way of painting: "Instead of painting things, he paints ideas."[3]

The conceptual Pont-Aven has no truck with Breton folklore or the regionalism that was growing in reaction to the triumphalist Third Republic, a movement with more than a hint of parochialism fed by an absurd desire for superiority. The place of Pont-Aven and Le Pouldu in the history of ideas and of artistic representation is assured. These villages have acquired universal significance—not a label that art historians have stuck on *a posteriori*, but an aura that impressed itself on the artists themselves when they settled or spent a few weeks there in around 1890. Everything around is saturated with sacredness. The art that was produced in these small houses and among these old mills has nothing to do with local colour, despite the carved clogs and headdresses, because Pont-Aven's universality is also a product of its history and traditions.

The museum of Pont-Aven has quite rightly titled an exhibition across two seasons, *Modernity in Brittany*,[4] eschewing the use of the awkward word "school." Every artist represented in the collection introduced his own type of modernity to the banks of the Aven, comparing it with others' contributions of course, but also contrasting it with a land that seems so distant—in time, in space, and in its legends. These artists intoxicated with modernity were in love with the exoticism of an area that seemed still to be in the Middle Ages—at the risk of further enchanting tourists, quick to be enthralled by folksy Breton ways. These "moderns" saw the cross carved onto the *menhir* of Kérangosquer, they walked along the path that climbs up to the chapel of Trémalo, with its yellow Christ, they sought models in the farms and inns, they rented boats and carts, they sometimes even learnt a little Breton, they lived in this inspired corner of Europe—to create talismans.

They all went to school. The artists represented here were all mindful of their schooling, which was mostly obtained in Parisian establishments that ought not to be regarded simply as straightjackets, which would have explained their desire to break away and catch the train for Quimperlé.

Émile Bernard briefly studied in the École des Beaux-Arts before entering the studio of Fernand Cormon. There is a story associated with the Cormon studio: it involves Van Gogh, who is said to have walked out before becoming properly acquainted. In a pioneering investigation inspired by Bruno Foucart and in several ancillary articles, Chang Ming Peng has shown that Cormon absorbed much of Alexandre Cabanel's subtle technique as well as Eugène's Fromentin's yearning for travel and new surroundings. His compositions, which have a certain power and novelty, introduce prehistoric man into history painting, depicting him hunting and fishing and conjuring up a kind of "primitive" beauty that had never been painted before. He portrays Victor Hugo's Cain from *La Légende des Siècles*, forever tormented by his conscience,[5] as well as the wandering peoples from bygone ages that were even then being discovered by the first scientifically trained paleontologists.[6]

The Cormon studio was above all cosmopolitan; it was full of pupils from all over the world, who dreamt only of setting off for China or Japan. Cormon was a professor at the École des Beaux-Arts and was elected to the Académie des Beaux-Arts in 1898, which put him at the very heart of the art establishment. He was in fact one of the most open-minded figures in the institute—and the young apprentices who made fun of him forgot what they owed to this first "school." Eric Forbes-Robertson, "John the Celt" as he was known in Pont-Aven, learned his craft at the Royal Academy School before discovering a freedom of sorts at the Académie Julian. He was captivated by the Bretons, whom he painted in their traditional costumes against a grey, almost abstract ground, where only a wooden table defines the space. The Académie Julian, whose rowdiness and carnival-like shows rivalled those of the École des Beaux-Arts, was in its own way another international melting pot and undeniably groomed its pupils to challenge for the Prix de Rome and to win competitions, but it had never been a doctrinaire prison. Several of the Pont-Aven painters were former pupils of the Académie Julian.

Émile Jourdan himself studied at the École des Beaux-Arts, before receiving further training from William Bouguereau and Tony Robert-Fleury. Henry Moret was taught to draw by Henri Lehmann, Ingres's successor—without being a strict Ingrist—and continued to learn, without turning a hair, with the purest of history painters Jean-Paul Laurens, a lover of legends and ancient tales and the illustrator of Merovingian exploits. It is also in this sense, too, that we should apply the word so frequently associated with the so-called Pont-Aven School: Synthetism.

This explains Paul Sérusier's portrait of Émile Bernard, seated in front of an imaginary view of Florence, probably painted in 1893 in Florence itself. These young artists shared a very strong sense of companionship—a sense of common purpose that was every bit as firm and multi-faceted as that of their counterparts in the Arts and Crafts movement in the 1860s or of the Pre-Raphaelite Brotherhood in the 1850s. The outline of Brunelleschi's dome in Florence was for them an emblem: they all dreamt of sparking a Renaissance. Modern Brittany was their fifteenth-century Tuscany.

Although they never made up a school, they all felt part of a movement whose creative energy was in no way inferior to that unleashed by the Medici's garden, to which Vasari gave legendary status. They believed in working together, exchanging views at what they felt was a new dawn of the human spirit, nourished by the noblest feelings—those nurtured in mystical Brittany, of course, but also others emanating from the immortal soul of Quattrocento Florence. Maurice Denis perpetuated this dream of an innovative circle of religious artists in his Ateliers d'Art Sacré, founded in 1919. But this was really no more than the continuation, *pace* the upheavals and revolutions in the art world of the late nineteenth century, of the impetus generated by the young artists in the studios of Ingres, the Flandrins, Amaury-Duval, and the German Nazarenes, who had all shared this dream of these Tuscan *arrière-pays*, where the painting of the "Primitives" had flourished like a gift of the landscape.

Sérusier's *The Talisman* lies at the heart of this "golden legend" of Pont-Aven, an idealised patch of land where everyone could dream together. While it is clear that *The Talisman at the Bois d'Amour*—of which there was more than one as far as the Nabis group was concerned—was never painted on a chocolate box, the story of this famous picture in the Musée d'Orsay serves as a parable because it establishes a dialogue. It is emphatically not a course taught by the head of a school to his pupil: "How do those trees appear to you? Yellow? All right, then, add some yellow. That tree is bluish, so paint it in pure ultramarine. Are those leaves red? Well, splash on vermilion."

The image of a discussion by the river, with replies worthy of Maeterlinck, seems almost redolent of Socrates teaching Phaedrus on the banks of the Ilissos—the subject of a sketch by Jules Moteley, dating from the same year 1888, depicting a woodland scene with a philosophical clearing, painted for a competition at the École des Beaux-Arts.[7] This story, so often trotted out, is too good to be true, but it encapsulates in just a few lines, recorded or invented by Maurice Denis, what must have so bewitched the painters of Pont-Aven, artist knights of the round table.

The Red Wood, painted on board by Sérusier in around 1895, is a "sacred wood," a temple of colours with Baudelairian "living pillars." Pierre Puvis de Chavannes had painted *The Sacred Grove, Beloved of the Arts and Muses* in the 1880s for the decoration of the grand staircase at the Museum of Fine Arts of Lyon; and at the end of the decade, he peopled the great amphitheatre of the Sorbonne with tall allegorical figures and philosophers. Sérusier's *The Red Wood* steers clear of bombast; it is just a musical variation on a red note, which has its green counterpoint—the colour contrast so dear to Delacroix—but he also prolongs the echo of Puvis's forest scattered with verticals and symbols. In *L'Œuvre*, written in 1886, two years before *The Talisman at the Bois d'Amour* was painted and four before the commentary provided by Maurice Denis, Zola describes a painting "lesson" that takes place not in Brittany among the jagged rocks of Pont-Aven, but in the countryside close to Fontainebleau, in an area littered with stones. A certain Claude, in whom Cézanne recognized himself, tries to convince Christine: "She had remained nonplussed now and then before a mauve ground or a blue tree, which upset all her preconceived notions of colour. One day when she ventured to express some criticism, about an azure-tinted poplar in this case, he made her observe nature and note for herself the delicate bluishness of the foliage. It was true enough, the tree was blue; but in her inmost heart she did not surrender, and rejected reality: there couldn't be any blue trees in nature."[8]

This excerpt from Zola's novel shows that these ideas were not so original after all and that escaping to the forest to paint from life and to seek out the primal purity of forms and the authenticity at the heart of painting was already an entrenched cliché in Paris. The fashionable studios were buzzing with talk of nature and sweeping away dusty conventional attitudes in the name of truth, observation and colour – incidentally, precisely Corot's approach in 1825.

The Goncourt brothers had also already sketched the outlines of this flight from the world, far from "beloved masters" and fine principles, in *Manette Salomon* in 1867. They had praised—not always ironically—this *école du plein-air*, which puts the artist at the heart of a primordial universe, looking to take as a model the jumble of rocks around Fontainebleau, which suggest the chaos that preceded the act of Creation—the world's birth and art's origin: "At that hour there was a magical atmosphere in the forest. Mists of greenery rose softly over the rocks, where the tender lightness of the tree bark died away, where the half-floating shapes of the trees seemed to lose their stiffness and bend with the nocturnal laziness of the vegetation . . . The blue tones and vaporous dimming of the evening increased imperceptibly . . . Wisps of fog began to drift by, smoke issued from a dream hanging in the air, pierced by the round, white-hot sun, casting all the flaming shafts of heaven's vault over the trees . . . Rembrandt's window, where there's a prism and where Shakespeare's Titania could play in a silver spider's web—all this was contained in that evening landscape."[9]

Is this, in a kind of back-to-front transposition of art, like a prose poem, the Goncourts's description of the "talisman" that their hero Coriolis, fleeing from the Paris of the Salon and of the École des Beaux-Arts, wanted to unearth in the heart of the woods, like a modern-day knight on his quest for the Holy Grail? Are Pont-Aven, the Bois d'Amour, the Pension Gloanec, and the Hôtel Julia mental constructs? Are they literary spaces to be discovered scattered between Shakespeare and Maeterlinck? Simple painterly pretexts, like Bastien-Lepage's peasant women, designed to launch artistic inventions on the Paris market that leant on Puvis and Ingres, while affecting to turn their back on them?

Certainly not. The village's instant appeal, with its promenades, fountains, rocks, and the natural amphitheatre at Le Pouldu a little further, offering a wonderful view of gathering storms, is a key component. But these features provide only the initial dazzle and are quickly followed by allusions to the Old Masters, references to others' work and the re-awakening of the cycles of the great legends. The *gouren*, Breton wrestling, which seems to have come down unchanged through the ages like the tournament games performed at Combourg witnessed by Chateaubriand as a child, interested Émile Bernard quite as much as Gauguin. However, his painting is a bout between colours applied in an abstract picture space—a blue roof is all it takes to create a landscape—haunted by Jacob's struggle with the angel painted by Delacroix for the Chapel of the Holy Angels in the Church of Saint-Sulpice.

The year before, Gauguin had brought his famous *Vision of the Sermon* to Pont-Aven. It is impossible not to compare the two works, if only on account of the geometry of the headdresses in the foreground. Gauguin concentrates on red tones, while Émile Bernard employs yellow as the dominant colour, which serves to turn the real into the abstract, the hill into an ideal "gold background." Real daily life in Brittany, observed at will, enabled both to build their own creation. The play of colours enables two different, neighbouring images to take shape, thanks to a magic transformation that has as much to do with geography as with history.

In 1888, Bernard painted *Three Breton Women in Widows' Bonnets*, a small work with a perfectly structured, geometric composition. There is no narrative content, no emotion in the depiction of these three women: the artist is only interested in the three "buildings" made of white cloth, strange shapes with fine pink and blue stripes. The shading and areas of flat colour create an abstract space where colour is paramount. Bernard was twenty at the time. This painting, in which he explores the fullness of the moment—as in *Buckwheat Harvesters* (Metropolitan Museum, New York) or *Harvesting in a Wheat Field* (Musée d'Orsay, Paris)—is perhaps his very own talisman, a profession of faith that deserves to be hung opposite Sérusier's *Talisman*, which was painted in the same year.

Five years later, Paul Sérusier would turn to the masters and traditions—in other words ,the secrets of Brittany. An island rises out of the green waves painted in *The Mammau*, or *The Fire Outside*, in 1893, which calls to mind the island of King Arthur. At a time when both England and France were in the grip of a passion for Celtic archaeology, it is impossible not to note the historicist aspect of this composition. A mysterious ritual is taking place here. The Gundestrup Cauldron had been found two years before in a peat bog in Jutland and the cauldron an old woman holds in her hand not only recalls the cauldron of the witches in Macbeth, which had inspired a print by Delacroix, it is also the physical representation of a mythical alchemy in a small painting combining the four elements—earth, air, fire, and water. The painting is also a plain and straightforward picture of a Breton woman in an apron holding a kitchen implement in her hand—and that's all it would be, an example of local colour, if it weren't for the procession of other women climbing the hill, with the slowness and solemnity of people about to worship in secret. The choice of matt colours evoking early Renaissance frescoes or the Italian Primitives contributes to this ambiguity. *The Mammau* is like a panel in a Breton predella whose full meaning escapes the uninitiated viewer

When Ferdinand du Puigaudeau paints Breton women around a fire on the beach at Le Pouldu, he plays with the area's quiet, poetic rituals, which are still so close to the ceremonies of medieval times. Like his first cousin Alphonse de Châteaubriant, a

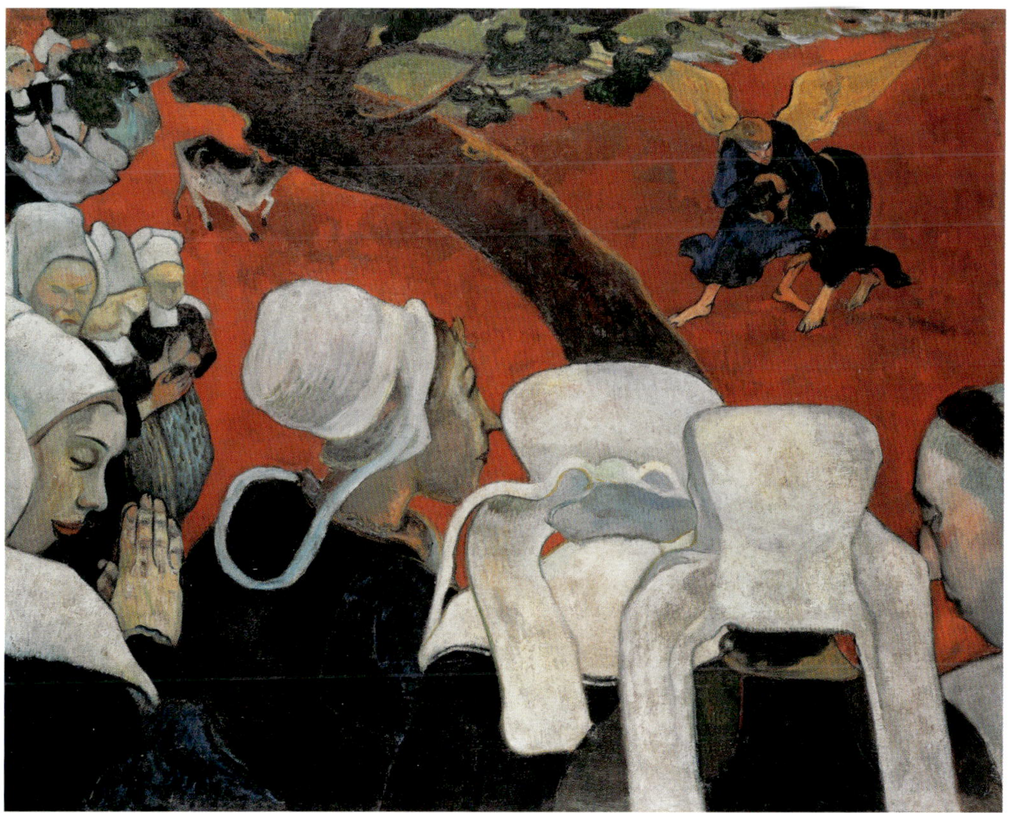

Paul Gauguin (1848–1903)
Vision of the Sermon
(or *Jacob Wrestling with the Angel*), 1888
Oil on canvas
73 x 92 cm
National Gallery of Scotland, Edinburgh

popular writer who later became a collaborationist, he was the embodiment of the impecunious gentleman artist who turns his hand to depicting the legends of his ancient land. The Combourg festivals described by Châteaubriand—a tutelary figure and near-namesake, with whom there was otherwise no connection—at the beginning of *Mémoires d'Outre-Tombe* had already acquired this undertone: the myth of the survival of customs in a land cut off from the rest of the world. The interest in Brittany this painting displays is of an ethnographic and romantic kind: these Breton women in their typical headdresses look like the sisters of the women of the desert that Odette du Puigaudeau, Ferdinand's daughter, set off to study in Africa in the late 1930s. For Ferdinand du Puigaudeau, this mysterious ceremony performed on a moonlit night, associated as it is with Le Pouldu, once a favourite haunt of Gauguin, Émile Bernard, and Charles Laval, is quite suited to an Impressionist sky whose shimmering sunset he extends here.

Pont-Aven is thus not a new "school" and neither does it represent a radical break with tradition. It attracted skilful artists who never totally rejected the training they received and had no particular desire to work alone. In her *Gauguin*, Françoise Cachin quite rightly stresses that Émile Bernard did not go to Brittany in the hope of finding a *tabula rasa*: "The presence [in Pont-Aven] of Émile Bernard, who was then just a talented young artist who had strong ties with the most philosophical and spiritualist Parisian symbolism . . . influenced Gauguin far more than the latter ever acknowledged . . . The pictures Bernard brought with him that he had painted the previous winter and the heated discussions his youthful enthusiasm generated in the Pension Gloannec were just the kind of stimulus Gauguin needed . . . "[10]

In a letter Gauguin wrote to "Schuff," his good friend Schuffnecker, which Fraçoise Cachin quotes later, he explodes this heady demiurgical self-importance—the artist is the Creator, the master of his world—which was echoed by Émile Bernard's Catholicism: "A word of advice: don't paint too much after nature. Art is an abstraction; draw it out of nature as you dream before it and think more about the creation that will result from it, it's the only way to climb towards God, by doing as our holy master does, by creating."[11]

Maurice Denis, who painted scenes from his life as if straight from the Gospels (his wife Marthe Denis inspired *Perros-Guirec, Jesus at the Home of Martha and Mary*) wrote to André Gide, who new Le Pouldu and its artistic milieu well, having arrived at dinner one evening in the inn run by Marie Henry, as he recalls in *Si le grain ne meurt*: "And here I am now, perhaps not the Fra Angelico, but at least the Flandrin or the Overbeck of my time . . . "[12] Maurice Denis is aware he is writing a sacred chapter in the history of an art he knows in intimate detail. Pont-Aven as the new Assisi? The cradle of fresh Nazarenes? The houses where the painters lived are like granite cells added to those of the Monastery of San Marco in Florence. It was no doubt so for Maurice Denis, and there's no question that the terrace of his house, Silencio, shown here in 1917, was perfect for daydreams. His wife Marthe died two years after this painting, which is a tribute to the Martha of the Gospel, she who did not choose the "better part." The painting became a talisman, a *memento mori*, for the artist, too.

But Gospel righteousness is not the only thing bubbling away in the Breton cauldron. Armand Seguin, the youngest of the group, sees far more in it: Baudelaire's *Artificial Paradises*, Paul Verlaine's face, the Inca profile of Gauguin that turns into that of a demon rivalling Orcagna's in Santa Maria Novella, and the red hair of a swooning green fairy. This wide-eyed devil also seems to have come out of a Japanese print. Is the composition, which looks like an illustration to place opposite a text, an amusing send-up? Jean-Jacques Henner, who loved to paint beautiful redhead, was elected to the Académie des Beaux-Arts in 1889; so, is Seguin trying to make fun of him? Or is the idea to portray all those he most admires in a brazier set in hell, in the eyes of the most god-fearing critics?

Armand Seguin contributed to the sense of companionship in Pont-Aven. He was friends with O'Conor and spellbound by Gauguin, but did not have the time to publish all that he wrote on the artists of Brittany, accounts which he as an engraver could have illustrated himself in the medieval sense of the term, his life being cut short at the age of thirty-four. Destitute and suffering from tuberculosis, he died in the house of Paul Sérusier, who had taken him in. Armand Seguin's etchings unquestionably have a place in any collection of talismans.

The miracle of the village of Pont-Aven is that each artist believes it was he who discovered it. Gauguin was the first to mention the village in a famous letter that has been endlessly quoted since John Rewald published excerpts in his *History of Impressionism*, in which he often humorously describes how he arrived in a hamlet already inhabited by painters with the intention of becoming their prophet: "I'm working hard and with success; I'm respected as the best painter at Pont-Aven: it doesn't earn me a penny more, it's true . . . At all events, it makes me respectable and everyone here (Americans, Englishmen, Swedes, Frenchmen) ask me my opinion, . . ."[13] Gauguin was the architect of a utopia; he turned Pont-Aven into the "somewhere, out of this world" where artists who had read their Baudelaire went to drink from the well, before the Marquesas.

Did they all forget Impressionism, then? What place did the previous wave's innovators have in the visual culture of those who went to Pont-Aven? The artists of Pont-Aven to a large extent defined themselves in relation to Gauguin, but they also knew the work of Monet, who at around this time stopped being regarded as an evil influence and reprobate and was mutating into the French master par excellence, admired from the United States to Japan.

The portrait of Louise Lançon, who married her cousin Schuffenecker, painted by Émile Bernard in 1888, is a kind of response. The figure is outlined with a thick black line and divides the composition in two. Some paintings can be made out on the wall on the right, while on the left a distant landscape seems framed just like the pictures. This window opens onto Impressionism, a landscape painted in light shades, with a vibrant stroke, but in all likelihood built up in the studio. Is this an example of synthesis or dichotomy? The Schuffeneckers, friends with Pissarro and Guillaumin, were at the very heart of the artistic life of the period.

En plein air painting, in the "Impressionist" manner, continued to be pursued in the countryside around Pont-Aven and by the sea. The small study titled *Red Rocks* dashed off on impulse by Roderic O'Conor is certainly a personal, visual "impression" that took form on the easel set before the landscape. There is no artificial foreground to give depth of field; the viewer's eye dives straight into the sea foam.

The Australian artist John Peter Russell had the good fortune to meet Monet, and the even greater merit to be appreciated by him. He was one of the young artists from all over the world that established the fame of the Cormon studio. He settled in Belle-Ile and like Monet he loved to battle against the elements, with his canvases and material, in the storm. In his house overlooked by the great Goulphar lighthouse tucked away in its cove at Bangor, he painted assiduously and received friends, one of the chief of whom was Rodin.

He painted a portrait of Van Gogh and caught the attention of Matisse and the Fauves, before fading from the limelight, from which he is now once again emerging. He continued to paint in the Impressionist style until late in life, prolonging the earliest impulses—evidence, if evidence were necessary, of how useless the label "neo-Impressionist" employed by certain art historians is. Impressionism existed in Pont-Aven and interacted with other forms that emerged from Symbolism and a certain academicism pursued by other means: these are neighbouring villages.

Henry Moret's villages are hard to identify and lack any distinguishing features. His *Fermes en Bretagne* (*Farms in Brittany*) suggests he saw Cézanne's *The Hanged Man's House* and that he studied Monet closely. He is steeped in Impressionist sensibility and "worked" for Paul Durand-Ruel. His *Chaumières en Bretagne* (*Cottages in Brittany*) are not just a soft option used cynically to entice Parisian, and soon American clients; he carefully composed, outlined and structured his paintings, perhaps mindful of his training at the École des Beaux-Arts.

La petite gardienne de vaches (*The Little Cowherd Girl*), painted in around 1904, is a successful example of the desire to continue in the Impressionist mode, while incorporating the latest trends. He renders the play of light on the Aven in a virtuoso display of technique, exhibiting all he learned from Pissarro to Seurat. The eye swirls around the young Breton girl in her headdress, an explosion of white, in a microcosm of colours that seem to encompass the whole of Armorica's nature. Henry Moret chose to explore the countryside, concentrating on the banks of the Scorff at Hennebont—in the same way as Constable was intoxicated by the banks of the Stour in the 1820s—seeking new subjects in nature to paint. Doëlan became his base.

His painting attempts to combine the never explicitly expressed principles of Monet's "Impressionist" style of 1874 and the geometrical study of form pioneered by Cézanne. This was an intellectual exercise that collectors fought over because they

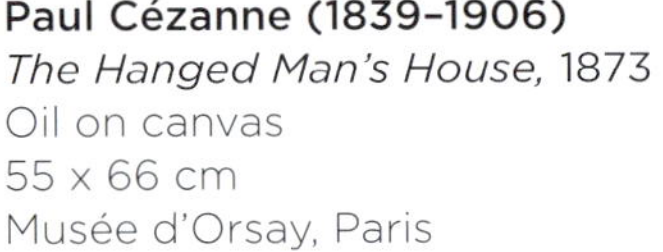

Paul Cézanne (1839–1906)
The Hanged Man's House, 1873
Oil on canvas
55 x 66 cm
Musée d'Orsay, Paris

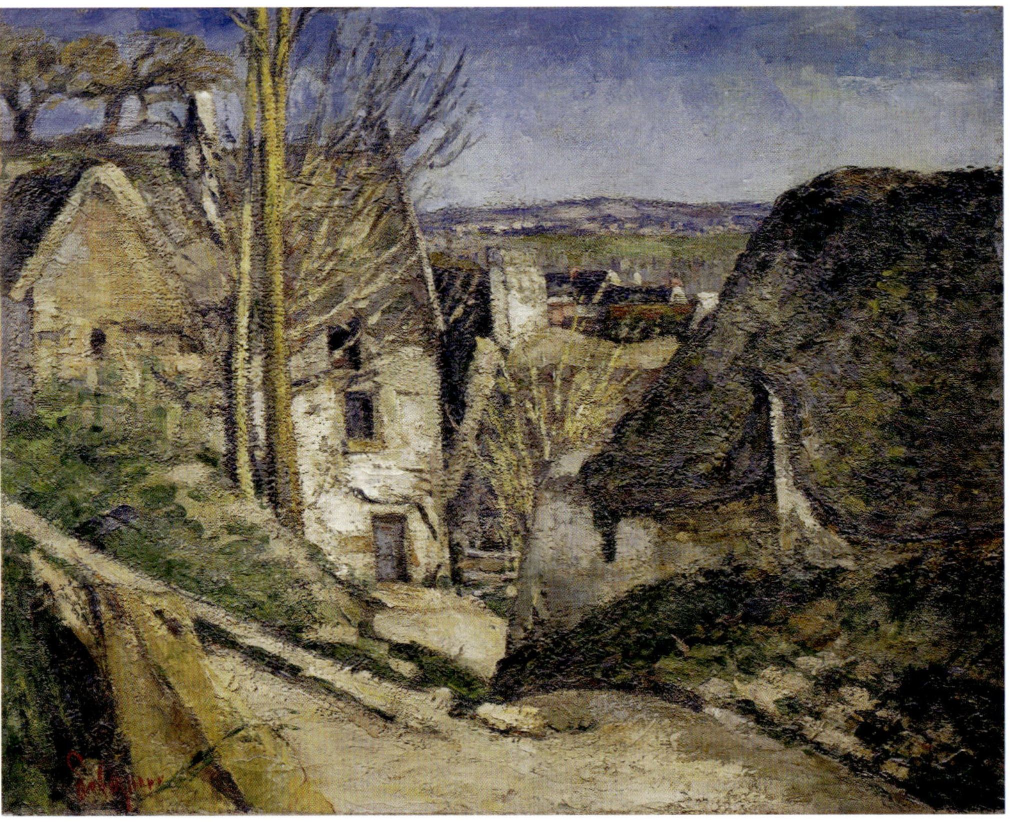

saw in it an unchallenging, domesticated modern art providing charming images of rural life in bygone times. In a rapidly industrialising France—Cormon went so far as to paint *Une Forge* (*A Forge*) in 1893—Moret continued to churn out visions of a prolonged easeful life appropriate for "tasteful" interiors, which collectors filled with eighteenth-century furniture. This is what lies at the heart of the misunderstanding that has long lain like a fog over a legitimate interest that these pleasant but at the same time well-structured compositions can elicit. They have fully earned their place among the "talismans" of Pont-Aven.

The Dutch artist Jan Verkade painted haystacks in 1891, at the same time as Monet. Is that enough to make him an Impressionist? His Cloisonné style marks him out as closer to Émile Bernard. The year he spent in Brittany was an important landmark in his career. He was able to pursue *en plein air* painting, without turning it into a rigid dogma. His haystacks are highly distinctive: standing out as they do against a field, they aren't, as in Monet, used to denote the season or to depict agricultural labour or the daily routine.

Émile Jourdan, who was Breton himself, painted his landscapes in sets and continued to work at combining Monet's innovations with the use of simplified, geometric forms owing very little to him, in paintings such as *Sardiniers sur la côte rocheuse* (*Sardine Fishing Boats by a Rocky Coast*), painted in 1914, or *Le port de Brigneau* (*Brigneau Harbour*), 1915. *Entrée de la rivière* (*Entrance to the River*), painted in 1926, testifies to the persistence of a Pont-Aven style within Pont-Aven itself in an artist who had witnessed the period of Gauguin and Bernard and who continued to give his pictures a strong structure built up through short brushstrokes, as if painting had come to a full stop in a village whose artists now attracted flocks of art lovers and imitators.

In Douarnenez, Maxime Maufra also worked in the open air, but since he had no formal training, he frames his compositions in the "classic" manner: his *Douarnenez, soir brumeux* (*Douarnenez, Hazy Evening*) is arranged around a gentle diagonal, with boats drifting in the distance in the soft evening light. Once again, in this skilful, meditated work, the careful balance in forms transcends the literal depiction of a landscape the artist knows well. The clear geometric construction of this composition goes hand in hand with an intuitive understanding of what, in the studios he never cared to enter, was known as "aerial perspective"—the poetry of a cloud-spotted sky sweeping into the distance, with mauve giving way to pale blue and the darkest blues are set off through the addition of white.

Brittany at the time of the wonderfully successful works of Moret and Maufra was in fashion. At the end of the nineteenth century it was also cosmopolitan, paradoxically because the whole world thought it was cut off. Costaérès Castle, on an island near Trégastel, had been built in grand medieval style by a rich Polish engineer, Bruno Abakanowicz, who built the Bellevue Hotel at Ploumanac'h. He received many of his compatriots at the castle, especially Henryk Sienkiewicz, who finished writing *Quo Vadis*, one of the most famous novels of the period, there. This sweeping, Catholic-inspired epic that aimed to evoke another vanished world, Ancient Rome, was published in 1896. Is he the sitter in Władysław Ślewiński's painting, in the guise of an architect sitting in front of his mock-up on a small stand? Ślewiński, a Polish nobleman who also studied at the Académie Julian and met Gauguin, concentrated mainly on still lifes as a way of experimenting with colour variations. Can the shapes and patterns on Ślewiński's blue plates on an orange tablecloth be said to be Impressionist? They can be compared with Meijer de Haan's still life painted in around 1889 contain-

Edgar Degas (1834–1917)
A Woman Seated beside a Vase of Flowers,
1865
Oil on canvas
73.7 x 92.7 cm
Metropolitan Museum of Art, New York

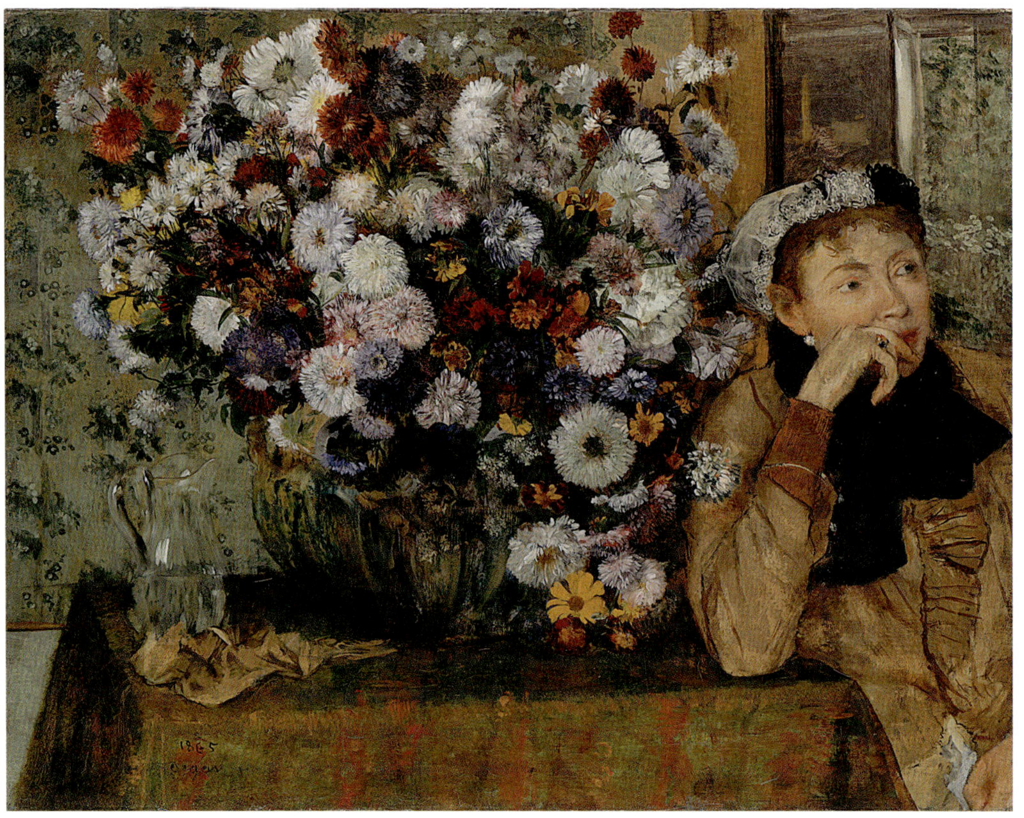

ing onions, a carrot, and a jug on a straw chair, where the artist employs blue to set off the other colours. Meijer de Haan visited the exhibition of work by the "Impressionist and Synthetist group" at the Café Volpini in Paris in 1889, where he discovered Gauguin, Bernard, and Schuffenecker, marking the start of a famous odyssey that would lead the Dutchman to lodge at Marie Henry's in Le Pouldu.

In 1885, one year before Gauguin moved to Pont-Aven, Stéphane Mallarmé published "Richard Wagner, rêverie d'un poète" in the *Revue Wagnérienne*. Paying tribute to the great composer, thanks to whom the public "marvels at seeing its own secret origins staged," he explores the legendary, abstract world the author of the *Ring* invented as a land and a hinterland, a complete world from the end of ages, which translates into music a chivalrous, enlightened tradition, using an utterly new and breath-taking idiom: "His gestures draw towards him our dreams of sites or Edens, which the theatre of the past engulfs in the vain pretension of containing or depicting them. He, someone! . . . Does a spiritual fact, the flowering of symbols, or their preparation, demand a place in which to develop other than the fictional focus of the crowd's gaze? Holy of holies, but all in the mind...then, in some supreme burst of light, which arouses the Figure that is No One, there converges every mimic gesture that Figure seizes from a rhythm provided in the symphony, and setting it free! . . .

Thus is the mystery accomplished.

The city, which provided a theatre for the sacred experience, sets on the earth the universal seal."[14]

How can our minds not conjure up this land bearing the universal seal, the Brittany of the prelude to *Tristan*, this poem by Mallarmé, "without any scent," when we observe Émile Bernard's *Young Woman in Kimono, Reading*, who is indeed faceless, a "Figure that is No One." She is opening a book. She is like a piece that has dropped out of a medieval stained glass window. She might be a Japanese woman and owes nothing to the artist's time in the Cormon studio and not much to conversations with Gauguin, but there is a suggestion of Degas's off-centre compositions—*A Woman Seated beside a Vase of Flowers* dates from 1865—and Van Gogh's bunches of flowers. This absent figure is present; she is both a portrait and an abstract construct, a young woman caught by happenstance in the artist's exploration. More perhaps than any other masterpiece in this collection can this work truly be called a "talisman."

1. Estelle Guille des Buttes-Fresneau rightly speaks of a school "that is uncomfortable being so described since there never was a school as such. On the contrary, Gauguin encouraged his friends to be as bold as they could", in *Pont-Aven, un musée, une collection.* Paris: Somogony editions d'art, 2010, p. 26.
2. Yves Bonnefoy, *L'Arière-pays.* Paris: Gallimard, 1972, p. 23, quoted in Poésie Gallimard, 2003.
3. Sylain Alliod, "Alexandre Mouradian, hérault de Pont-Aven", *La Gazette de l'hôtel Drouot*, no. 28, July 14, 2017, p. 18.
4. See Estelle Guille des Buttes-Fresneau and Hervé Duval (eds.) *La Modernité en Bretagna*, vol. 1, *De Claude Monet à Lucien Simon 1870-1920* and vol. 2, *De Jean-Julien Lemordant à Mathurin Méheut, 1920-1940.* 1940. Milan-Pont-Aven: Silvana Editoriale-Musée de Pont-Aven.
5. Chang Ming Peng, "Fernand Cormon's Cain: Epic Naturalism in Nineteenth-Century History Painting," in Petra ten-Doesschate Chu and Laurinda S. Dixon (eds.), *Twenty-First Century Perspectives on Nineteenth-Century Art, Essays in Honor of Gabriel Weisberg*. Newark: University of Delaware Press, 2008, p. 238–46.
6. Chang Ming Peng, "Fernand Cormon et le grand décor: l'exemple de l'amphithéâtre du Muséum d'Histoire naturelle de Paris (1893-1897)", *L'Atelier*, bulletin no 8 of Association Le Temps d'Albert Besnard, 2013.
7. In the collections of the École nationale des beaux-arts (Ensba).
8. Émile Zola, *L'Œuvre*, preface by Bruno Foucart. Paris: Gallimard, "Folio" series, 1983, p. 184.
9. Edmond and Jules de Goncourt, *Manette Salomon*, preface by Michel Crouzet. Paris: Gallimard, "Folio" series, 1996, pp. 337–38.
10. Françoise Cachin, *Gauguin*, 1958, new revised edition. Paris: Le Livre de Poche, 1989. p. 72.
11. *Ibid.* p. 73.
12. Letter dated July 11, 1999, *André Gide – Maurice Denis, Correspondance, 1892-1945.* Paris: Gallimard, 2006, p. 147.
13. John Rewald, *Histoire de l'impressionisme*. Paris: Hachette, "Pluriel" series, undated, pp. 346–47.
14. Stéphane Mallarmé, *Écrits sur l'art*, ed. by Michel Draguet. Paris: Flammarion, 1998, p. 367.

CATALOGUE

ESTELLE GUILLE DES BUTTES
DIRECTOR AND CHIEF CURATOR MUSÉE DE PONT-AVEN

Émile BERNARD (1868–1941)

Three Breton Women in Widows' Bonnets, 1888
Oil on canvas
25 x 31 cm

Bernard was only twenty when he painted this extremely daring study. The artist approaches the triple portrait in a totally free, unexpected way, breaking completely with academicism and the often picturesque standard depictions of rural Brittany.

Three figures—shown in profile, full-face, and three-quarter views—stand out against a uniform though rather poorly discernible green ground. They are the only elements that together build the "landscape format" composition. The painter audaciously truncates the figures in the manner of the Japanese printmakers as if to set them more forcefully before the viewer. And in accordance with the still embryonic Synthetist style, they are all outlined by a strong blue line that sharply encloses the white, blue, and orange colour fields. The painter concentrates on the essential components of his subject without being distracted by details: he is less interested in facial features than in the angle at which the heads are held and is clearly captivated by the long side folds of the headdresses sweeping down over the women's shoulders. This type of headwear is the typical attire of Breton women in mourning. A sense of depth is suggested by a group of women in the background—small, un-detailed figures depicted in black and white seen from behind.

That same year Émile Bernard painted one of his most famous works in Pont-Aven: *Breton Women in a Meadow* (Private Collection). This painting marks a turning point both in Bernard's artistic development, as he breaks away from all conventions, and in the history of art itself. Working closely with Paul Gauguin, Bernard laid the foundations of the Pont-Aven School, giving free rein to the impulses of modernity and paving the way for the Expressionism that was to come. Besides being striking in its freshness and unaffectedness, this small painting of women in mourning also has an impressive pedigree. Bernard first gave it to his friend Charles Filiger, who was associated with the Pont-Aven group, swapping paintings already being common practice among artists. It then passed into the hands of Marie Henry, who ran the Buvette de la Plage inn in Le Pouldu, and was inherited by her daughter Léa, before being acquired by Dominique Denis, the son of the "Nabi of the beautiful icons." It is now one of the most emblematic works in Alexandre Mouradian's collection.

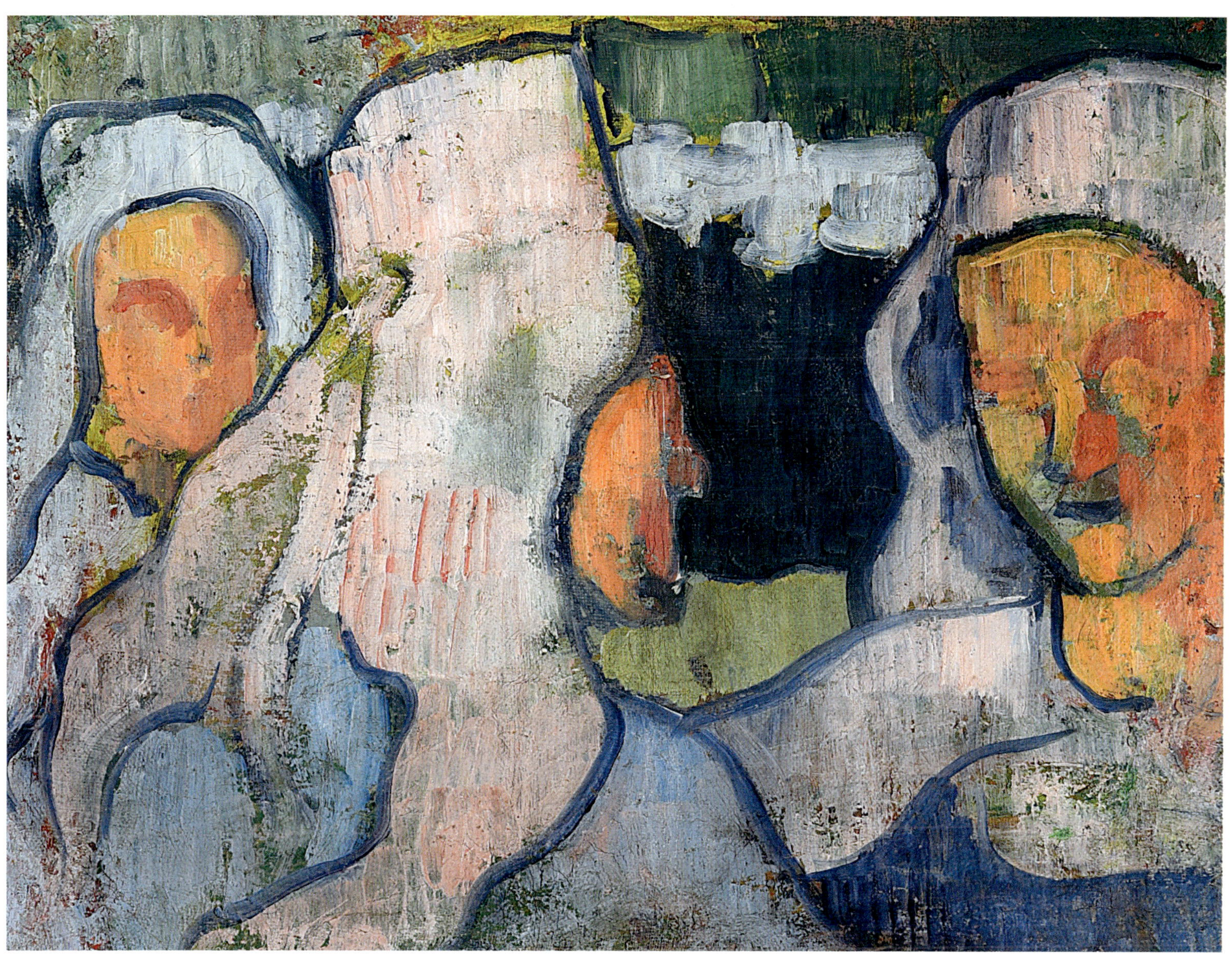

Émile BERNARD (1868–1941)

Portrait of Madame Schuffenecker (Louise Lançon), 1888
Signed and dated on lower left
Oil on canvas
66 x 54 cm

The model for this work, Louise Lançon, was the wife of one of Émile Bernard's closest friends, Claude-Émile Schuffenecker (1851–1934), whom he met at Concarneau at the end of the summer of 1886 and later encountered again in Paris. Far from being merely a good likeness of his friend, this portrait by Bernard is above all a successful depiction of her personality, taste, and modern spirit, as the clothes she has chosen to sit in explicitly suggest. She is portrayed in three-quarter view, inviting us to note the landscape in the background—depicted in an Impressionist style—seen through an open window. The skilfully structured composition is built around the traditional vanishing point running from Madame Schuffenecker's back to the houses in the distance and exploiting a section of the room's wall decorated with two paintings and the vase of flowers on the windowsill.

In contrast to the standard classical approach to the representation of space and depth of field, the treatment of the face and body, adding a dark, emphatic though restrained outline, is a good example of the new style of painting Émile Bernard began to adopt after 1887 as he attempted to develop a synthesis of competing styles. The portraits Bernard painted in 1887 and 1888 well illustrate the different influences on the artist just as Impressionism was drawing to a close and Cloisonnism began to rise in popularity. Like his close colleagues Gauguin and Van Gogh, he was also powerfully swayed by the discovery of the Japanese print, with its highly stylized, striking motifs.

Émile Bernard painted another portrait of Madame Schuffenecker in 1888.

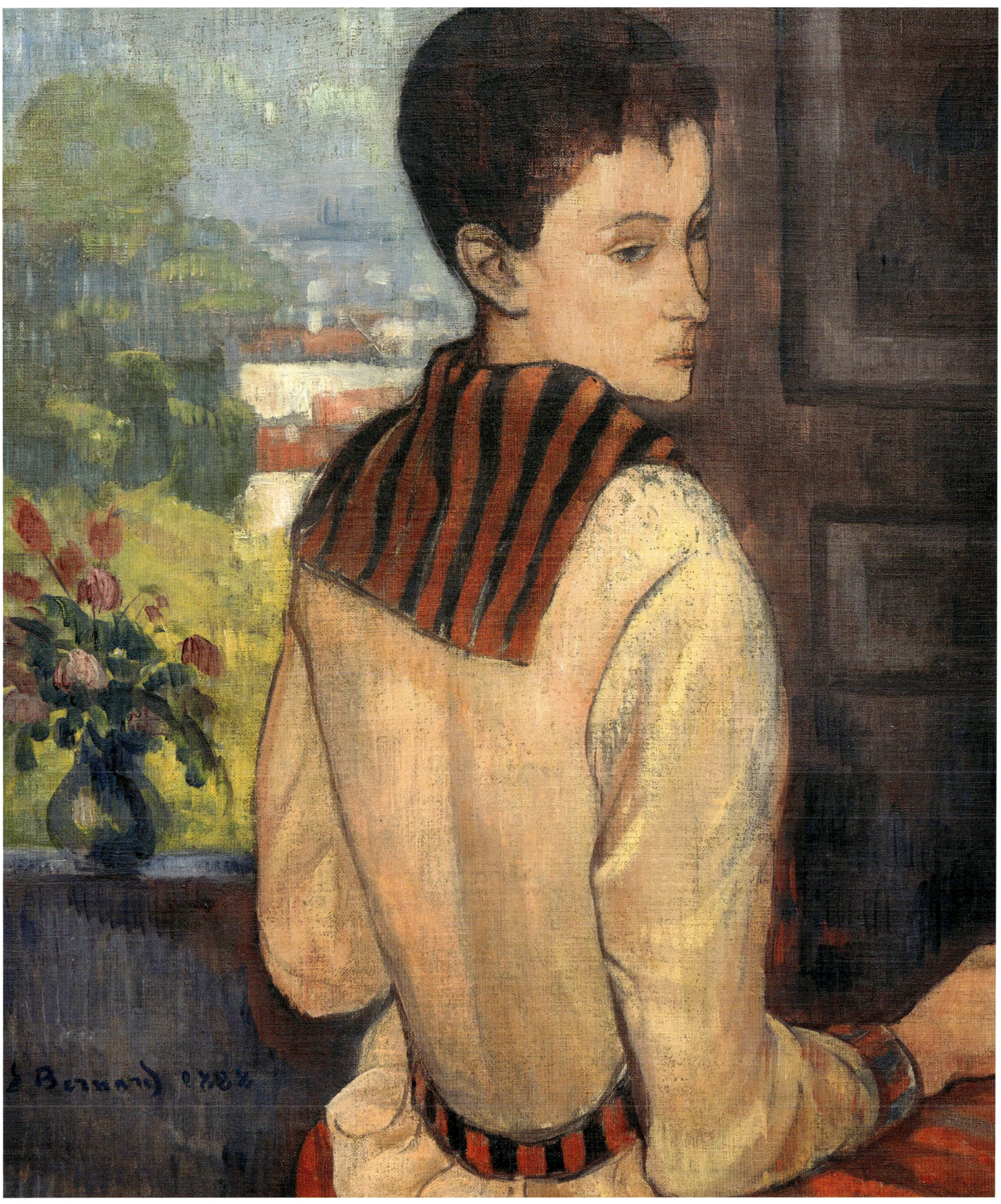
Bernard 1888

Émile BERNARD (1868–1941)

Young Woman in Kimono, Reading
Undated and unsigned
Oil on paper mounted on canvas
40 x 50 cm

Born in Lille, Émile Bernard moved to Paris with his family in 1881. Displaying a rare talent for drawing at a young age, he joined the Cormon studio in 1885, where he met Toulouse-Lautrec and Anquetin. In 1886, the young Émile discovered the village of Pont-Aven in Finistère. His conversations with Paul Gauguin gave rise to two major Synthetist works from 1888: *Vision after the Sermon* (or *Jacob Wrestling with the Angel*), now in the National Gallery of Scotland in Edinburgh, as regards Gauguin, and *Breton Women in the Meadow* (or *Le Pardon*), now in a private collection, painted by Bernard. The Pont-Aven group would henceforth coalesce around these two men, until they quarrelled in 1891.

This half-length depiction of a female model with one arm resting on a table seems to be an opportunity to experiment a style, in which primacy is given to mood rather than traditional figurative representation. Even if the figure's facial features are totally absent, the black lines and the areas of flat colour enable us effortlessly to conjure a graceful, thoughtful profile, her head turned slightly downwards over the book in her hands.

Japan was in fashion at the time and artists liked to have their models pose with the attributes of the Land of the Rising Sun, as illustrated in this case by the kimono: the fabric's pattern is just barely suggested in order to make the areas of flat colour stand out.

The sober composition is skilfully structured, with a firmly geometrically defined tablecloth in the foreground, whose sharp angles are counterbalanced both by the sinuous forms of the woman's outlines and by the ornamental effect of the vase and its exotic flowers. This carefully considered treatment of form is matched by a highly restrained palette gravitating around three hues: yellow for the table, mauve for the woman, and green for the wall.

Émile Bernard was one of the founders of the Pont-Aven School and this work is a powerful statement of his commitment to Synthetist aesthetic principles.

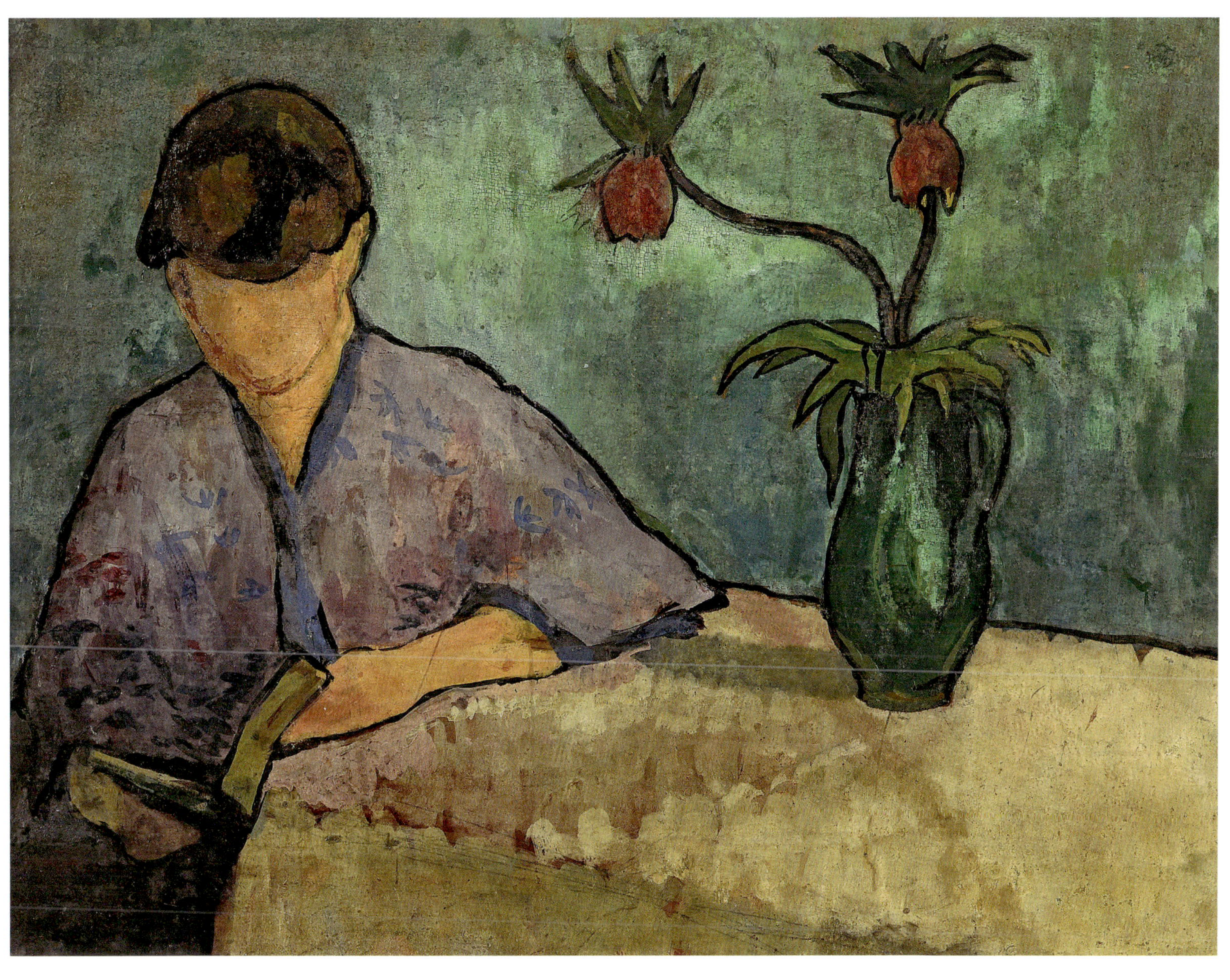

Émile BERNARD (1868–1941)

Breton Wrestlers, 1889
Signed and dated on lower right
Oil on canvas
80.7 x 65.5 cm

Émile Bernard takes up one of the favourite themes of the Pont-Aven School: Breton wrestling (*gouren* in Breton). Paul Gauguin was among those who depicted this sport in *Breton Boys Wrestling* (1888, Private Collection). In the nineteenth century, this lay amusement often took place after Confession. The aim is to force one's adversary to the floor, with both shoulders touching the ground at the same time. Only a few holds were permitted in this local form of wrestling.

While the foreground is occupied by Breton women wearing Pont-Aven head-dresses, shown from behind and from the side, the viewer's eye is immediately drawn to the two men in a clinch beyond them. A church steeple and the outlines of the roof of a house suggest the existence of a village at the foot of the hills in the distance: this might be Pont-Aven itself, since Bernard was never far away at this time. Indeed, Breton wrestling bouts in Pont-Aven were traditionally held in the Lollichon field above the church.

This sketch, striking in its modernity, was dashed off quickly with no respect for academic conventions. Eschewing any attempt at modelling, the artist pares the figures down to their very simplest form, applies flat colour over large areas, like the yellow ground that acts to hold the whole composition together, and introduces daringly extreme experiments in foreshortening. The two small cows are completely out of scale compared with the human figures depicted right next to them, revealing a completely new approach to how spatial relationships and depth of field are treated.

Bernard was a keen admirer of Japanese prints and he borrowed from them the idea of painting half-length figures to give them more presence. This normally means the top part of the figure, but the three dresses truncated at the waist at the top of the picture help us to envisage other onlookers, women and young girls, arranged in a circle around the wrestlers.

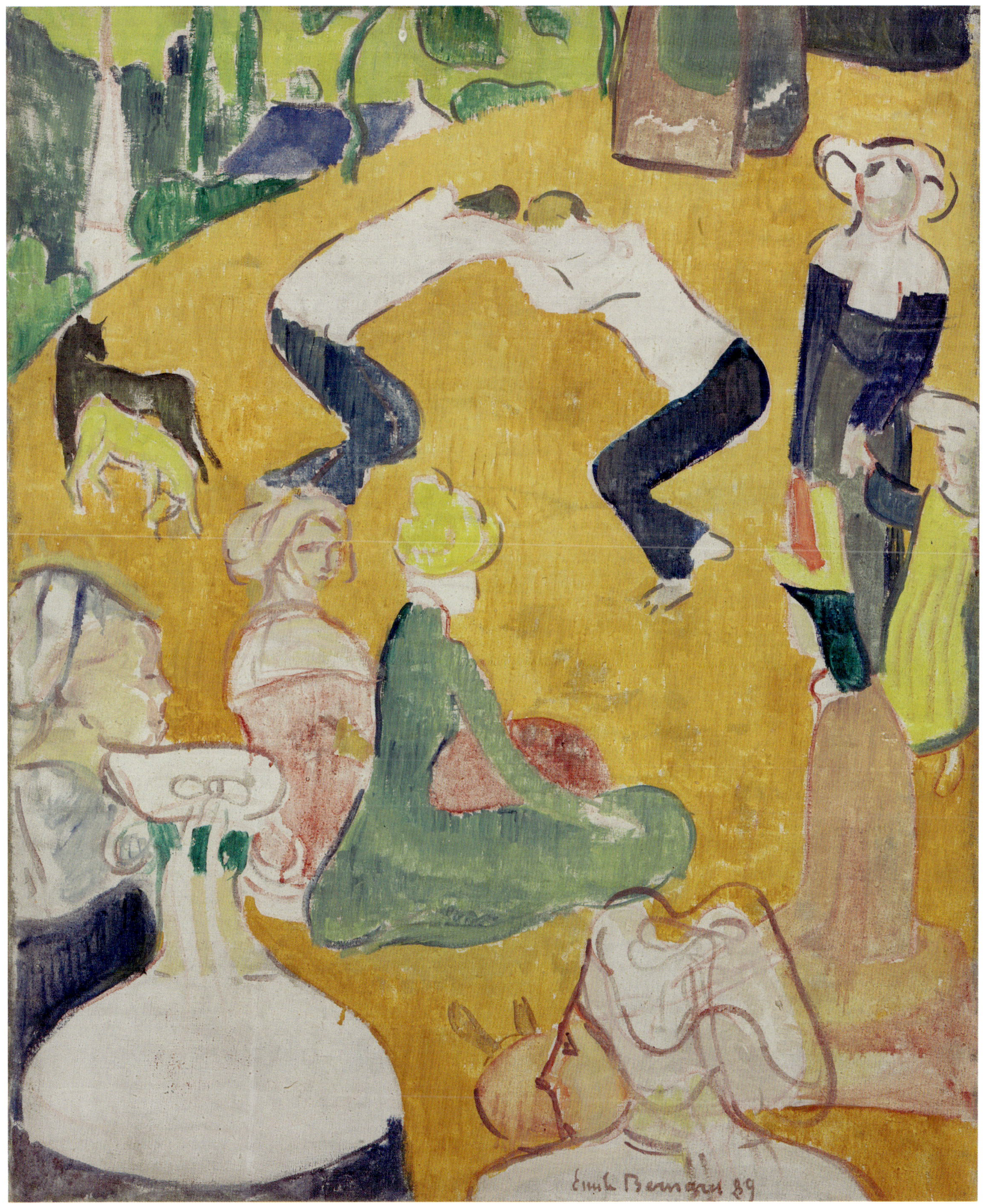
Emile Bernard 89

Meijer DE HAAN (1852–95)

Nature morte, oignons, carotte et pot (*Still Life, Onions, Carrots and Jug*), circa 1889
Unsigned
Oil on canvas
34 x 41 cm

Born in Amsterdam to a Jewish family of biscuit makers, Meijer de Haan arrived in France in 1888, taking no further part in the family business. The following year he discovered Synthetism in Paris when he visited the Café des Arts run by Monsieur Volpini. The exhibition held there from June 10 to November 6, 1889, titled *Exhibition by Painters of the Impressionist and Synthetist Groups,* included several works by Bernard, Gauguin, Laval, and Schuffenecker. It was an opportunity for these artists to set themselves apart from their established colleagues at the Universal Expo.

Up to then, Meijer de Haan had been painting portraits and genre scenes in chiaroscuro, taking his cue from the great Dutch masters such as Rembrandt. But he altered his technique after meeting the artists from Pont-Aven and Le Pouldu, especially Gauguin, whom he considered his mentor. He adopted the same simplified line and pure colours while exploring ways of depicting light.

Doing away with perspective, in this painting he assembles a jug, a carrot, and four onions on a straw-bottomed chair. The blue background, intersected by the strong diagonal of the chair, is reduced to a minimum so as to focus the viewer's attention on the still life itself. In such a small painting it also serves to make the objects taken from daily life loom larger. In this respect, the painting bears comparison with *Botte d'ail et pot d'étain* (*Heads of Garlic and Tin Ewer,* circa 1889–90, Musée des Beaux-Arts, Rennes) and *Nature morte avec pot, oignons, pain et pommes vertes* (*Still Life with Onions, Bread, and Green Apples,* circa 1889–90, Musée de Pont-Aven).

Meijer de Haan returned to Holland in 1891, where he met a premature death. He left most of his works to Marie Henry, with whom he had a daughter Ida, in Le Pouldu.

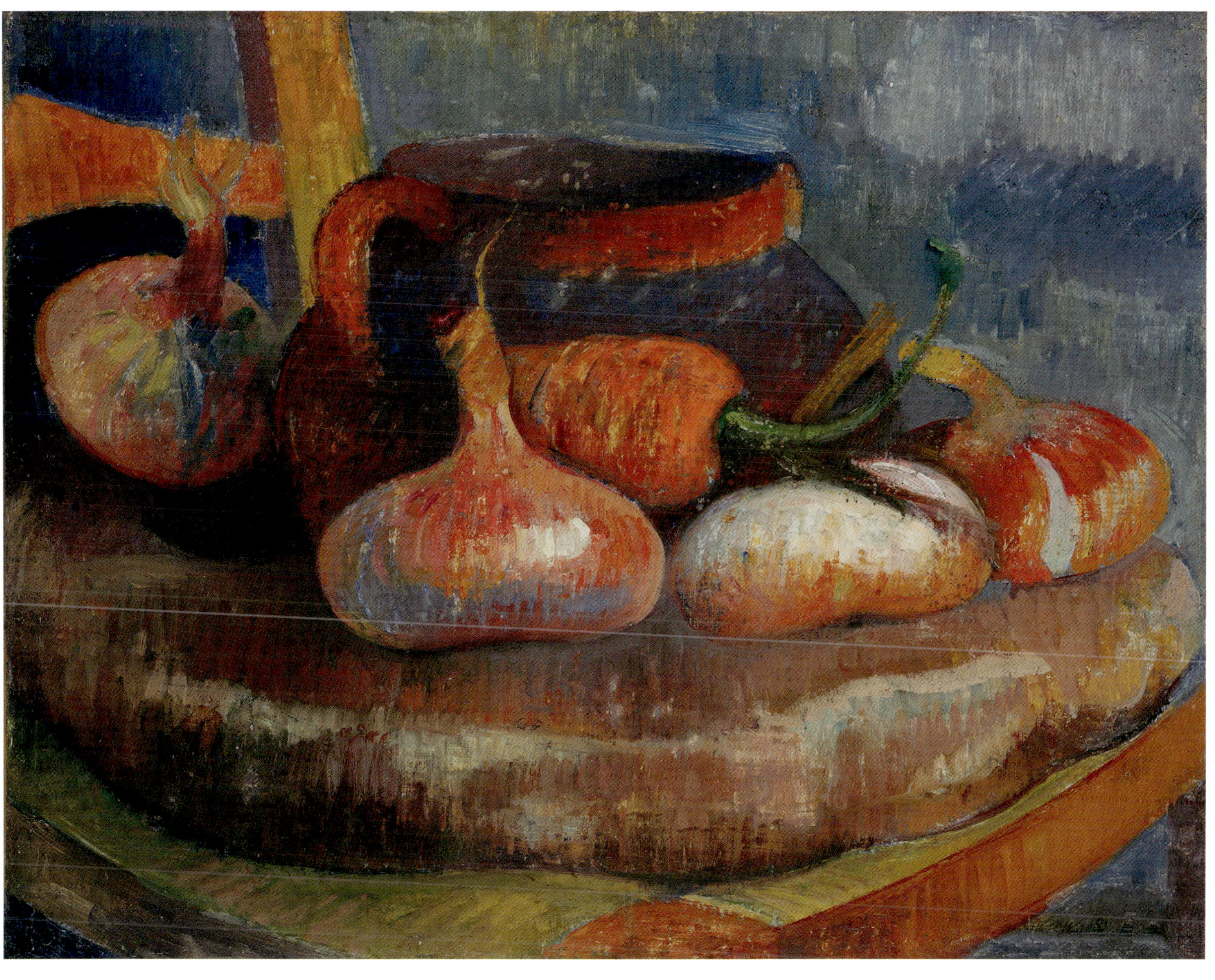

Eric FORBES-ROBERTSON
(1865–1935)

Jeunes Bretons de Pont-Aven
(*Young Breton Boys of Pont-Aven*),
1892
Signed, dated, and located
in Pont-Aven on lower right in red
Oil on canvas
100 x 73 cm

Eric Forbes-Robertson was born in London to an artistic family and began his training at the Royal Academy School in 1883. He moved to Paris in 1885, where he completed his training at the Académie Julian. Following in the footsteps of fellow artists who were enchanted by Brittany, he travelled to Pont-Aven in August 1890, probably encouraged by his friend James Henry Donaldson. He stayed a little over four years and during that time he became close friends with Paul Gauguin, Armand Seguin, and Alfred Jarry, while also enjoying a good relationship with Émile Jourdan and Maxime Maufra. He can be seen in several photos of residents of the period.

While his youthful works are distinguished by their sharp break with academicism, he very quickly made common cause with the Synthetists. The painting shown here straightforwardly depicts two children in their everyday clothes and wooden clogs. In spite of his subjects' humble appearance, the artist lends them considerable dignity by having them fill the picture plane and by enclosing them in a gentle circle of light. The detailing is well observed, especially in the little girl's hood and the boy's Breton waistcoat with its copper buttons. The bluish background features multiple diagonal striations, subtly suggesting the artist was not uninfluenced by the Divisionist technique.

In spite of his admiration for Gauguin, Forbes-Robertson was able to forge his own style, as this exceptional painting amply demonstrates. Other paintings in the artist's oeuvre confirm his interest in depicting childhood, not just as a focal point for a picturesque scene but as a subject in its own right, in all its consequence.

After pursuing a career in painting in Paris until 1900, Forbes-Robertson gradually drifted away from art and turned to acting, becoming a film actor in England under the pseudonym John Kelt—not so different from the nickname of "John the Celt" he had been given in Pont-Aven.

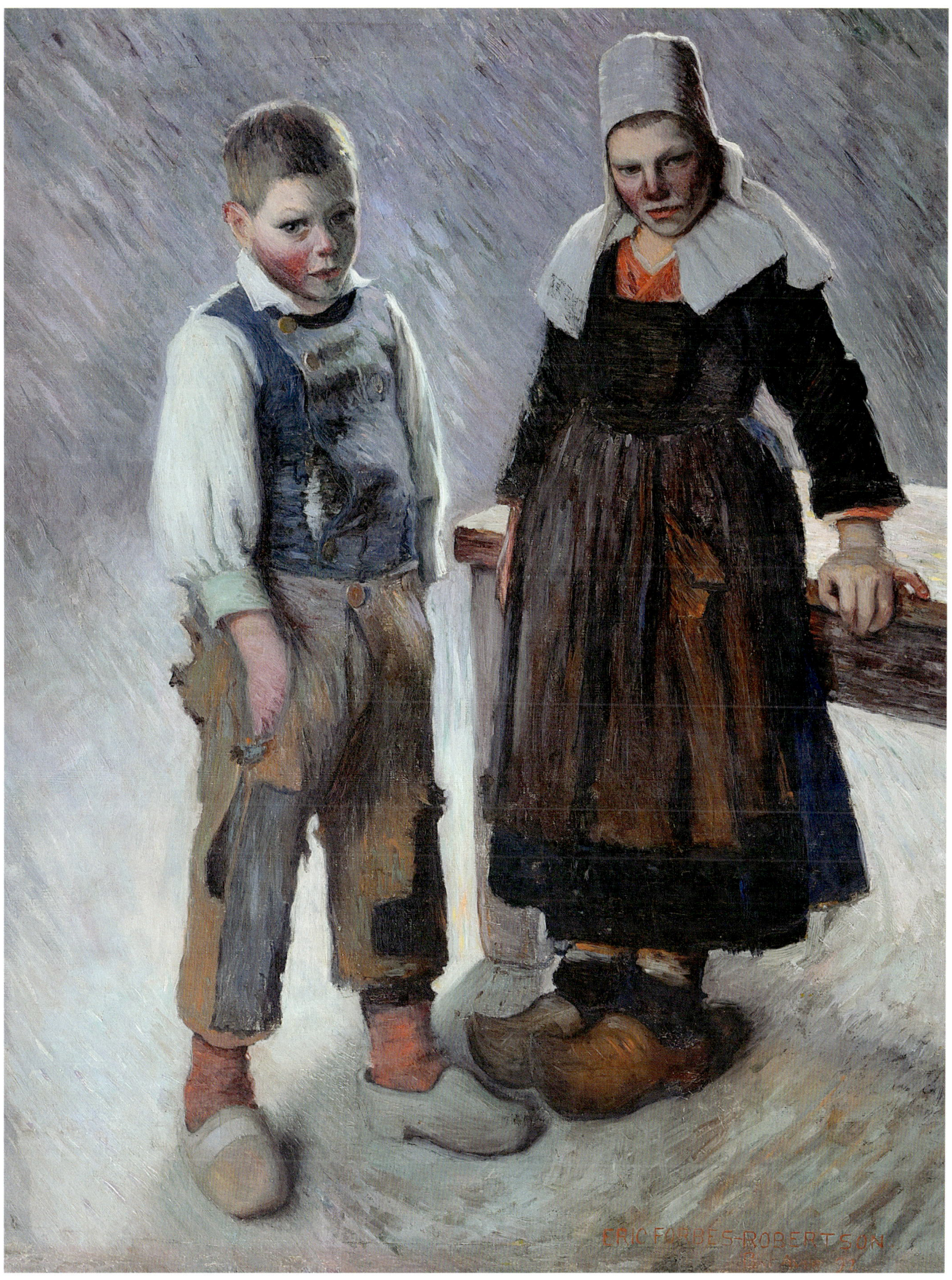
ERIC FORBES-ROBERTSON

Émile JOURDAN (1860–1931)

Sardiniers sur la côte rocheuse (*Sardine Fishing Boats by a Rocky Coast*), 1914
Signed and dated on lower right
Oil on canvas
97 x 107 cm

The son of a ranking customs officer and the grandson of a magistrate, Émile Jourdan was born in Vennes and entered the École des Beaux-Arts in Paris in 1880. Here he received a sound academic training, first under William Bouguereau, then under Robert-Fleury. He was a good student and at the same time attended classes at the private Académie Julian, where he was *massier* (head boy). He completed his studies in 1886 and probably took his first trip to Pont-Aven in 1888. There he met Paul Gauguin and became his friend and "disciple." Indeed, Gauguin mentions in a letter in 1889 that he is working together with Jourdan, confirming their close understanding.

Jourdan had already painted fishing boats in 1888, in his *Le Départ des Sardiniers* (*Sardine Fishermen Setting Sail*), and would do so many times again. Like the Impressionists, he enjoyed returning to the same theme time and time again to explore different approaches.

This landscape is a good example of how Jourdan manages to convey on the canvas the subjective experience of observing a scene: the subject becomes the vector of the artist's reverie. His choice of colours reveals a committed decorative stance. After 1910, his paintings begin to take on darker hues, like the dark blue he uses to depict the sea. The spatial layout exploits a linear network of arabesques reminiscent of the technique of Japanese engravers, such as Hokusai. All things Japanese were the fashion and Jourdan had been an admirer of Japanese prints since his years in Paris.

Never leaving Pont-Aven from 1888 until his death, Émile Jourdan kept to the margins of the art world. He did not exhibit at the official salons nor at the exhibitions organized by Paris galleries. On the other hand, he fostered close relations with artists coming to southern Finistère, especially Filiger, Moret, and Sérusier, all of whom were part of the Pont-Aven group.

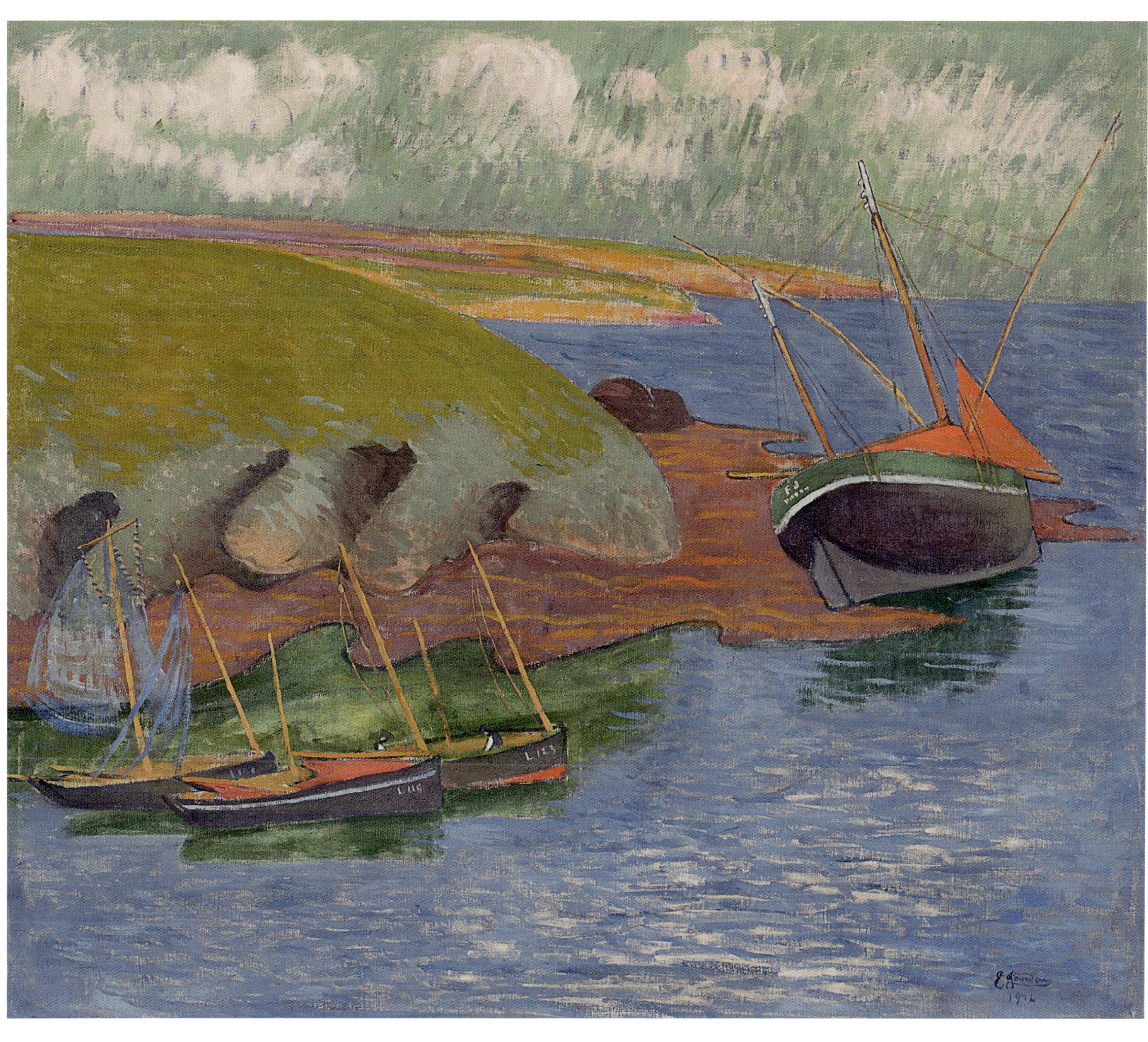

Émile JOURDAN (1860–1931)

Le port de Brigneau
(*Brigneau Harbour*), 1915
Signed and dated on lower left
Oil on canvas
73 x 60 cm

In terms of productivity, Émile Jourdan did not paint much and destroyed a lot. He was a perfectionist when it came to his work and was rarely satisfied with what he achieved. As a result, this is one of the very few works to have survived. Between 1911 and 1920, he often went to Brigneau, staying at the Auberge de la Mère Bacon, where he became friendly with the painters Maurice Asselin and Jacques Vaillant. Consequently, Brigneau harbour in Finistère was one of his favourite subjects.

Espousing the new aesthetics developed by Paul Gauguin and Émile Bernard, he simplifies the harbour's features. As often occurs in his pictures, there are no superfluous details and he lends some movement to the composition by simply adding some fishing boats. Form is underlined by a heavy outline. In the background, the houses are rendered schematically as white cubes or rectangles. The artist uses colours for their intrinsic value, playing on the harmonic range of pink/orange/blue/green, which is very uncommon for the period. Each plane is given a dominant tint, applied in a tight grid of parallel strokes, each defining space or underlining depth. The combination of concentrated effect of colour and stylization of form make this work a highly emblematic example of decorative Synthetism.

Known as "the painter of light," Jourdan rubbed shoulders with the writers Roland Dorgelès and Pierre Mac Orlan in Brigneau.

Jourdan's artistic reputation has developed gradually. He achieved national recognition when the curator Jean Cassou purchased *Rain at Pont-Aven* for the Musée National d'Art Moderne in Paris in 1955. This work is now in the Musée d'Orsay and on loan to the Musée de Pont-Aven.

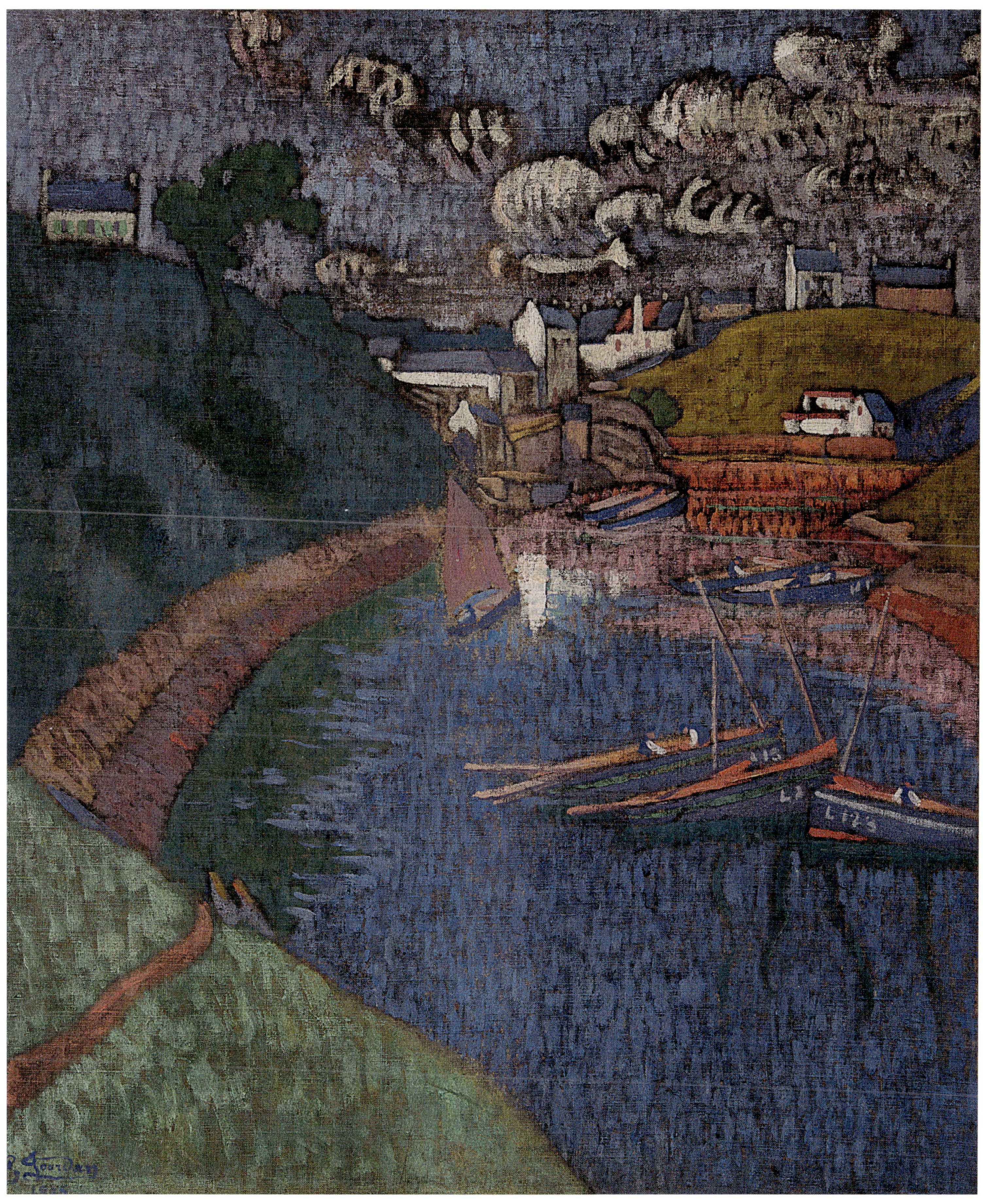

Émile JOURDAN (1860–1931)

Entrée de la rivière (*Entrance to the River*), 1926
Signed and dated on lower left
Oil on canvas
46 x 55 cm

Émile Jourdan lived in Pont-Aven for over forty years. By 1926 he was one of the artists who had done most to extend the aesthetics of the Pont-Aven School for as long as possible. What seems to engage him most keenly as he develops his recurring themes is the arrangement of form and the play of colours.

As in many of Émile Jourdan's works, the sky and the landscape intermingle. The painting's unity also depends on the carefully judged choice of dominant colours and the repeated parallel and slanted brushstrokes. In the background, a castle can be made out against the sky. This might be the castle of Hénan on the Aven. Scudding clouds and the boats' red sails lend vibrancy to the composition.

Having devoted his entire life to art, Émile Jourdan died in the Quimperlé hospice in a state of total destitution. In 1968, his children took his ashes back to Pont-Aven.

He is certainly one of the most neglected Pont-Aven artists and was really only reintroduced to a broader public in 1966, thanks to the twenty-six works displayed in the *Moret-Jourdan-O'Conor-Ślewiński* retrospective held in his native Vannes on the initiative of the curator Henri de Parcevaux. But it wasn't until his first solo retrospective held in the Musée de Pont-Aven in 1987, with fifty-six catalogued works, that he was brought to the attention of the general public.

This work was one of those displayed in the museum as number forty-two in the catalogue, titled *L'Aven à Hénan* (*The Aven at Hénan*). It is very close to *Ramasseurs de coquillages sur les bords de l'Aven* (*Shell Gatherers on the Banks of the Aven*), which belonged to the great collector of the Pont-Aven School Samuel Josefowitz.

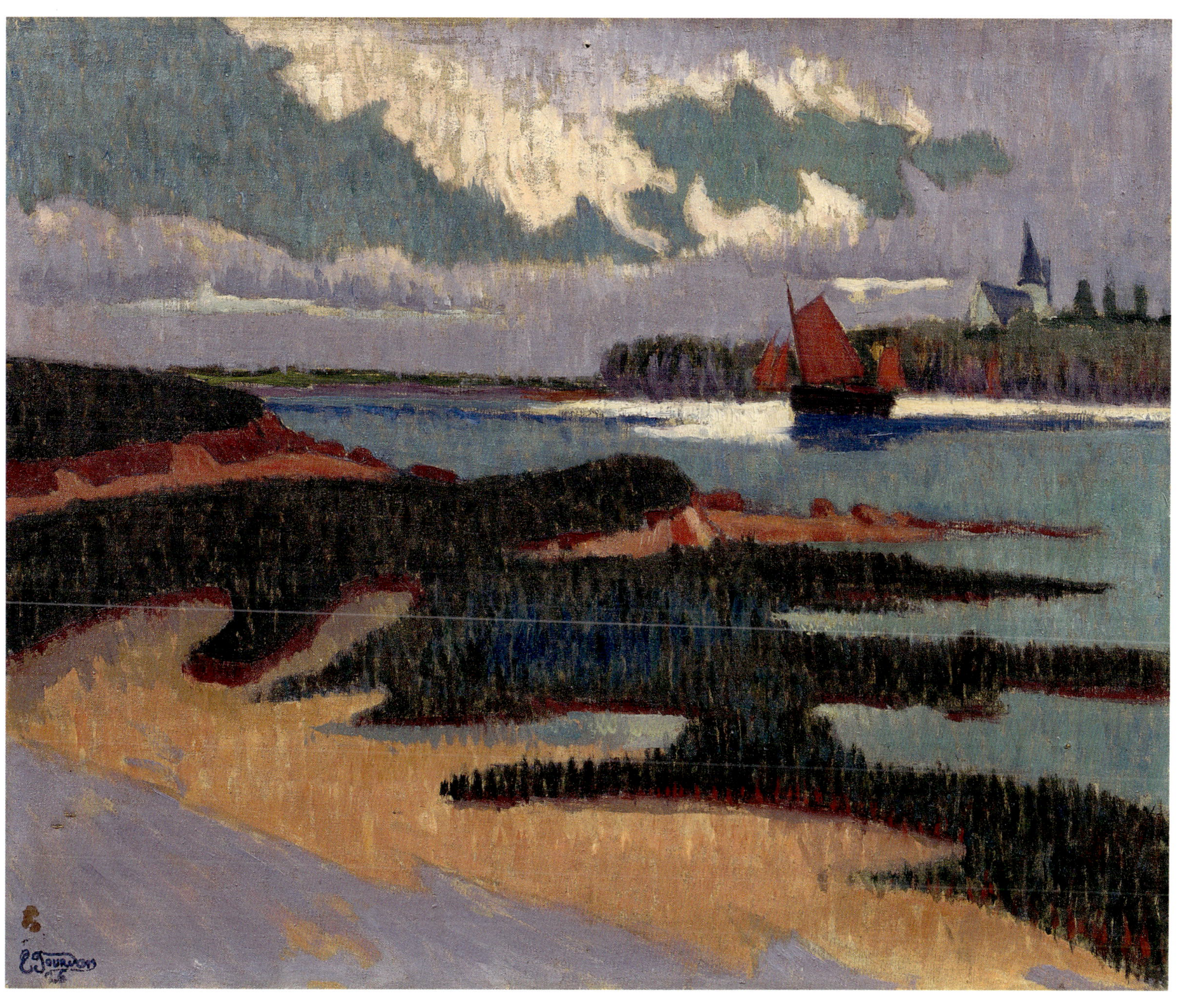

Maxime MAUFRA (1861–1918)

Douarnenez, soir brumeux
(*Douarnenez, Hazy Evening*), 1897
Signed on lower right
Oil on canvas
54 x 65 cm

Maxime Maufra was born in Nantes and discovered he had a gift for drawing during secondary school. In 1890, he abandoned his attempts to build a career in business and starting painting in earnest under Leroux and Leduc.

Adopting Émile Zola as his model, Maufra takes nature as his chief source of inspiration and pinpoints his stance in this observation: "What is an artwork? A corner of nature through a temperament." He worked hard to find his own voice by painting from life around Nantes, but it was only when he reached the Breton coast that his talent was at last able to flourish. This was particularly true of the southern stretch of coast, such as the Quiberon Peninsula and the famous bay of Douarnenez.

He was a self-taught landscape artist, learning his craft by observing the changing sea. But the time he spent in Pont-Aven and Le Pouldu were also fruitful. After meeting Gauguin, Maufra as well started to explore the potential of synthesis. As a result of his encounter with other artists and his studies from nature, Maufra developed his own personal style, a sort of third way. This painting represents a meeting point between Impressionism and Synthetism. Like the Impressionists, the artist depicts a precise moment, the day's close, and renders the mood with short brushstrokes. At the same time, he concentrates on simplifying forms, whether they be the coastline, buildings, or boats. The influence of Japanese prints is implicit in the stylised treatment of the trees.

Gauguin dedicated a pastel colour study, *Two Breton Women,* now in the Musée de Pont-Aven, to Maufra, writing: "To my friend Maufra, to an avant-garde artist," a rare tribute by the Pont-Aven master to a contemporary. The dealer Durand-Ruel was instrumental in getting Maufra's work known in Paris and the United States.

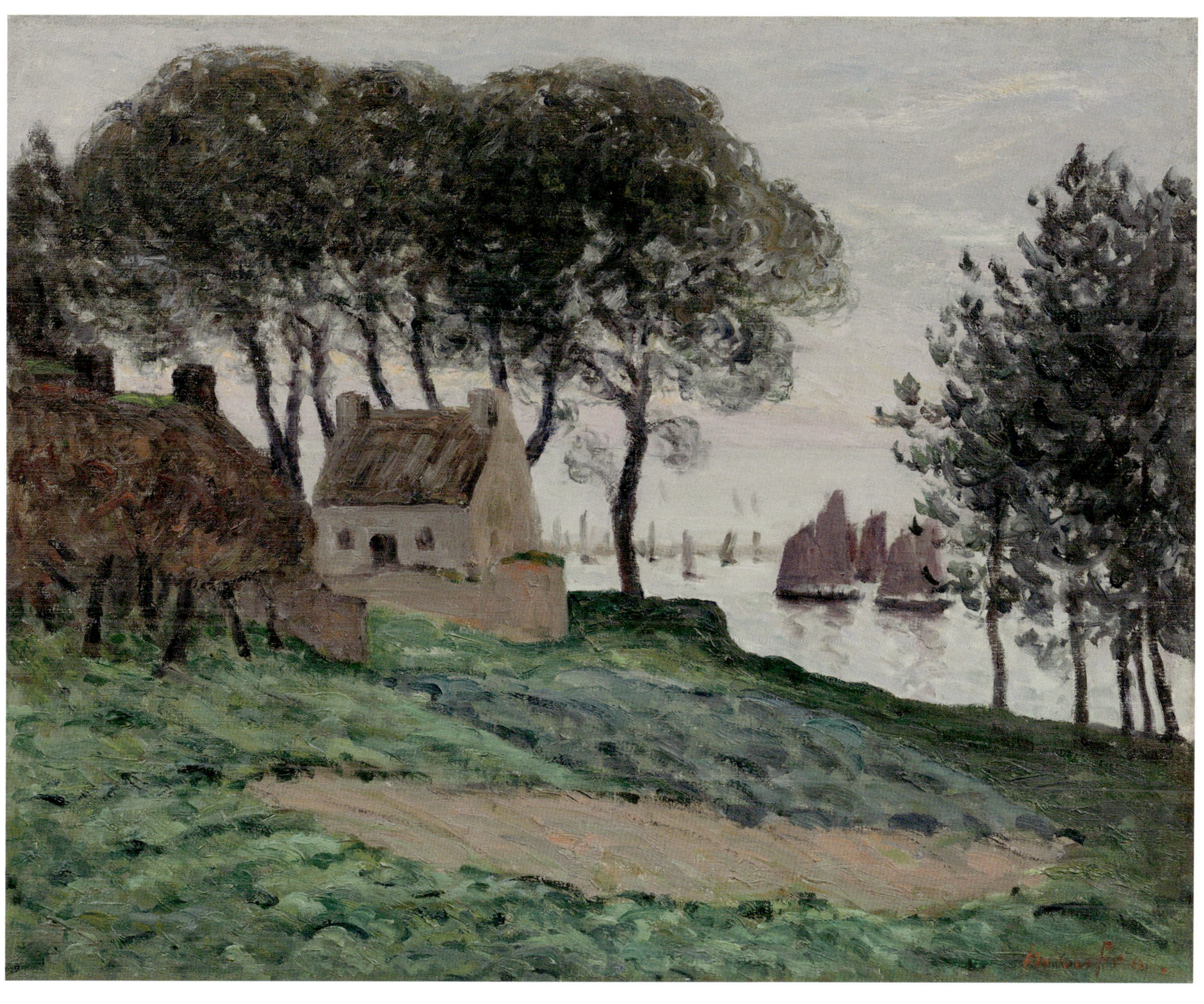

Henry MORET (1856–1913)

La petite gardienne de vaches
(*The Little Cowherd Girl*), circa 1904
Signed on lower right
Inscription lower right: L'Aven
Oil on canvas
45.5 x 64 cm

From 1882 Brittany was foremost among Henry Moret's favourite painting locations. In 1888, he met Paul Gauguin and the other artists gathered at Marie-Jeanne Gloanec's inn. While for a time following the new principles introduced by Bernard and Gauguin, he nonetheless regularly included his works in the exhibitions of Impressionists and Symbolists held at the gallery of Le Barc de Boutteville in Paris. This was part of a gradual drift away from the Pont-Aven School towards a closer association with the Impressionists.

In illustrating a scene from everyday life, the artist has taken care to pinpoint the location on the lower left of the canvas: "l'Aven" [The Aven], the Aven being one of the rivers he most frequently depicted. Both the girl, wearing her traditional headdress, and the cow are no more than patches of colour acting as focal points attracting the viewer's eye. And indeed, the way Moret builds up his composition with small dabs of colour reflects his espousal of Impressionist theories. This means that Moret's real aim is not so much to depict a little peasant girl in the countryside as to capture a fleeting moment in paint by reproducing the vibrations of the light on the canvas.

Émile Bernard well understood Moret's approach since he was once close to the Synthetists. Indeed, in *Le Nouvelliste* from August 20, 1939, René Maurice records Bernard's comments regarding Moret: "I held Henry Moret in great esteem and we would sometimes go for a walk together to look for subjects . . . I lost touch with him when I left Pont-Aven. He had turned [*sic*] from our experiments in Synthetism in favour of Monet's work *en plein air* and this was a considerable surprise to me. I had great respect for what he brought to the group and I thought he would continue along the same path. When I returned from the East after an eleven-year absence, I saw his paintings at Durand-Ruel's and I must say I was impressed. Far from wasting his talent, he had reinforced it by steering clear of theories and sticking close to nature, to life itself."

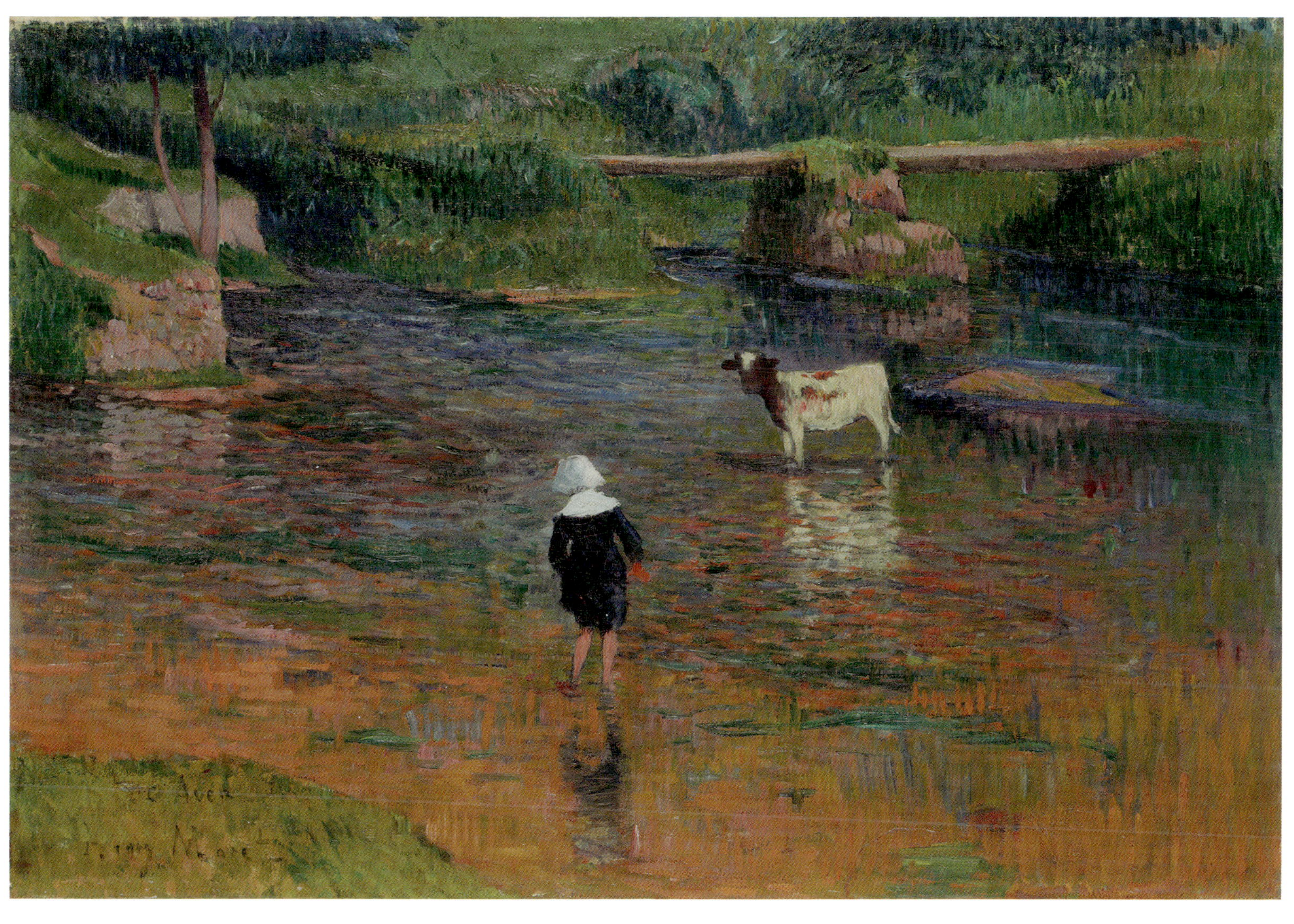

Henry MORET (1856–1913)

Fermes en Bretagne
(*Farms in Brittany*), circa 1905
Signed on lower right
Oil on canvas
73 x 60 cm

Henry Moret was born in Cherbourg and entered the École des Beaux-Arts in Paris in 1876 under Henri Lehmann. He completed his training between 1880 and 1883 with Jean-Paul Laurens, a specialist in large history paintings. After his first encounter with Paul Gauguin in 1888 and continuing to seek inspiration in the Breton countryside, Moret gradually worked his way back to an Impressionist approach. From 1894 he adopted Doëlan, in Finistère, as his base and explored the effects of the light in his new surroundings. The landscape depicted in this painting might correspond to the countryside near the harbour, where there were several farms. He liked to work in the open air, gathering sketches he could use for his pictures.

Moret's short, comma-like brushstrokes are typical of the Impressionist style, but several of his paintings also reveal his attempts to find common cause with Synthetism, something that makes him stand out among his peers. Between 1894 and 1896 he can be said to have found a perfect balance between the two approaches. The same applies in this instance, where the modelling of the farms displays his interest in simplifying form and applying colour for decorative effect, while the surrounding vegetation and sky are treated in an unambiguously Impressionist manner to convey all the vibrancy of the light. This convergence of influences and techniques can also be seen in a painting in the Musée de Pont-Aven titled *Rochers au bord de l'Aven* (*Rocks by the Bank of the Aven*), dating from around 1891.

Moret was fortunate enough to have his talent recognized by the gallery owner Durand-Ruel, who is renowned for having discovered many Impressionists. They had a very close understanding and their collaboration, which began in 1895, continued right up to the artist's death. The dealer is believed to have bought around 650 paintings by Moret. In 1898, Durand-Ruel organized a solo exhibition in his New York gallery, ensuring Moret would always be highly popular with American collectors.

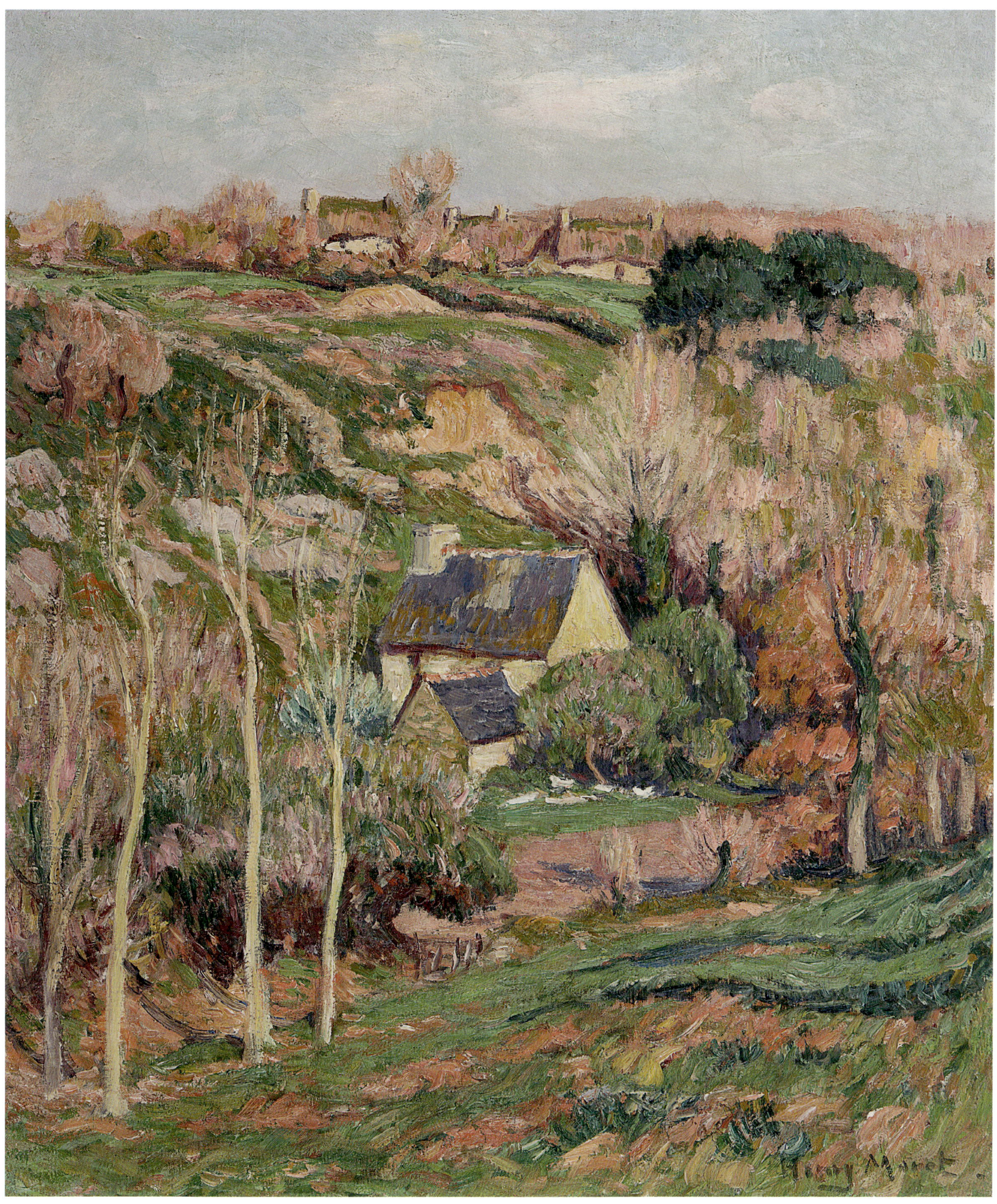

Henry MORET (1856–1913)

Chaumières en Bretagne, couleurs d'automne, (*Cottages in Brittany, Autumn Colours*), 1899
Unsigned
Oil on canvas
54 x 65 cm

Henry Moret discharged his military service in Lorient in around 1875, when he met Ernest Corroller, a local artist specializing in seascapes. While instructing Moret in his technique, he also developed in him a taste for working *en plein air.* Back in Paris, Jean-Paul Laurens ensured he had a counterbalancing command of academic painting.

In this painting, Moret underlines what he owes to Synthetism by emphasizing firmly structured compositions. The farms and the haystack are all confidently picked out and the solid outlines are then filled with countless short and even strokes of colour, in the Impressionist manner. As Claire Sauvage writes in the catalogue of the exhibition of his work held in the Musée de Pont-Aven in 1988: "Until 1909 Moret worked in a structured Impressionist style," a description that well expresses Moret's approach.

One of the reasons Moret was drawn back to Impressionism was that he befriended artists, such as Ernest de Chamaillard and Maxime Maufra, who were themselves painting in this manner. Ever observant, Moret produced a very considerable oeuvre in a career spanning thirty-three years.

In 1959, Henry Hugnault wrote in the preface to the Moret exhibition at the Durand-Ruel gallery: "Henry Moret is the whole of Brittany; Brittany is the whole of Henry Moret." And indeed, the artist spent most of the year in Brittany, even though he would return to his studio on Rue Milton in Paris from time to time.

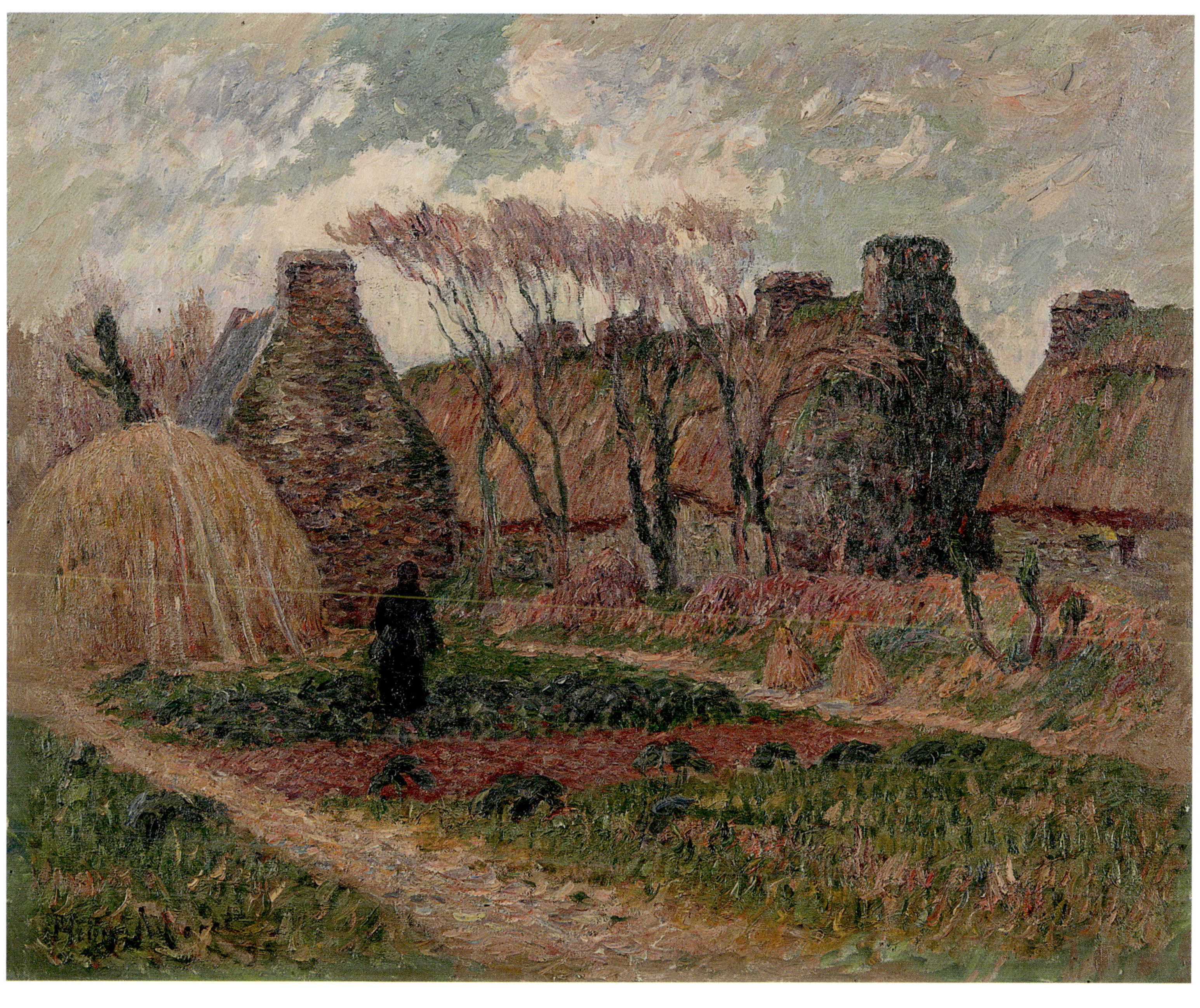

Roderic O'CONOR (1860–1940)

Red Rocks, 1898
Unsigned
Oil on canvas
54 x 65 cm

Roderic O'Conor, the son of a justice of the peace, was born in Ireland. He initially trained at the School of Fine Arts in Dublin from 1879 to 1883 and subsequently at the Académie royale des beaux-arts in Anvers. In 1887, he moved to Paris and probably discovered Pont-Aven in the same year, lodging at the Pension Gloanec. He returned frequently to the small Breton town from 1891, meeting Paul Gauguin, Ernest de Chamaillard, Charles Filiger, Armand Seguin, Paul Sérusier, and the Polish artist Władysław Ślewiński, who became his friends.

Breaking with his original training, the painting of the mature O'Conor, such as this example, displays striking energy, with bright, sharply contrasting colours applied across large areas of the canvas. In the foreground, the glowing rock stands out against the dark blue sea beyond. The flowing lines reinforce the decorative and expressive nature of the work. Just like *Yellow Landscape, Pont-Aven* (1892, Tate Gallery, London), this seascape does not attempt to provide a faithful representation of the scene before the artist, but rather a subjective interpretation of the impact it had upon him, with the stress being laid on the unleashing of the powerful forces of nature. In this respect, O'Conor adheres to the artistic values defined by Paul Gauguin. The site perhaps lies on the southern coast of Brittany, as we know O'Conor returned to Pont-Aven and Le Pouldu in the summer of 1898.

These same principles can be discerned in his etchings. It is worth noting that O'Conor's most powerful works date from his period in Brittany and the present painting is an excellent example.

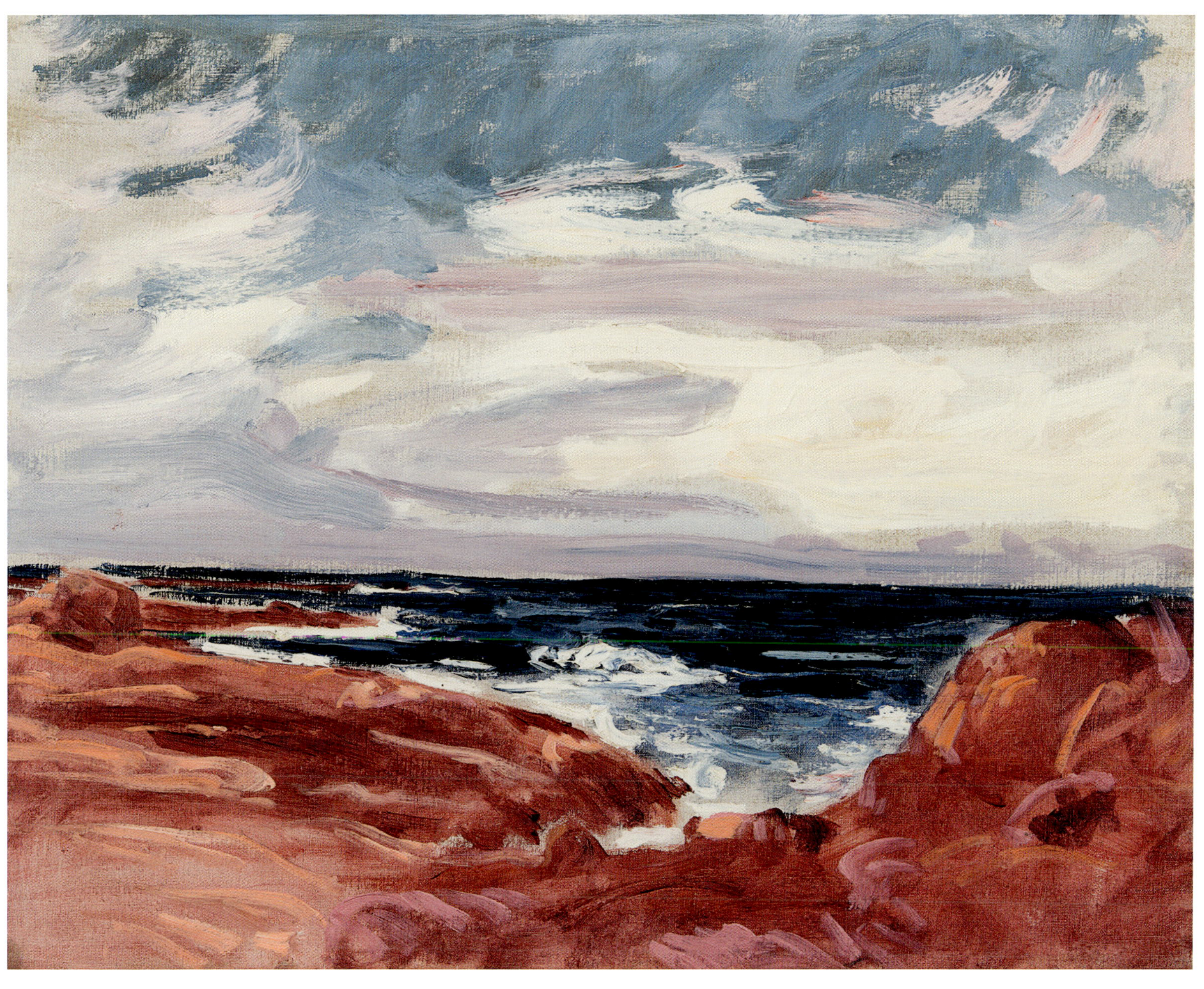

Ferdinand Loyen du PUIGAUDEAU (1864–1930)

Le Pouldu, le feu sur la plage (*Le Pouldu, a Fire on the Beach*)
Undated
Signed on lower right
Oil on canvas
60 x 81 cm

Born in Nantes into a family of landowners who had fallen on hard times, Ferdinand du Puigaudeau did not attend art school; instead, he obtained his education by travelling in Italy, Belgium, and Tunisia and by visiting museums. The self-taught artist visited Pont-Aven in 1886, where he associated with Paul Gauguin, Charles Laval, Émile Bernard, and Achille Granchi-Taylor. Ferdinand du Puigaudeau exhibited at the Salon of the Société Nationale des Beaux-Arts, in Paris, for the first time in 1890, then appeared regularly at the salons of Paris and Nantes from 1891. He lived in Pont-Aven with his family from 1895 to 1897 and in 1907 the family moved to Croisic, where Ferdinand rented the manor house of Kervaudu and entertained his painter and writer friends.

While remaining faithful to the Impressionist style, taking a particular interest in capturing effects of the light and nocturnal atmospheres, he is nonetheless closely associated with the painters of the Pont-Aven School.

The night scene depicted here shows a group of Bretons sitting and gazing into a fire on the beach of Le Pouldu. The flames lend warm yellow tones to the sand, creating a contrast with the cold blues of the sea and sky, which occupy two-thirds of the composition. The moon plays a key role in the painting, brightening the sky and creating reflections in the sea.

The artist's exceptional visual memory enabled him to repaint the same scene over and over again, introducing variations for effect.

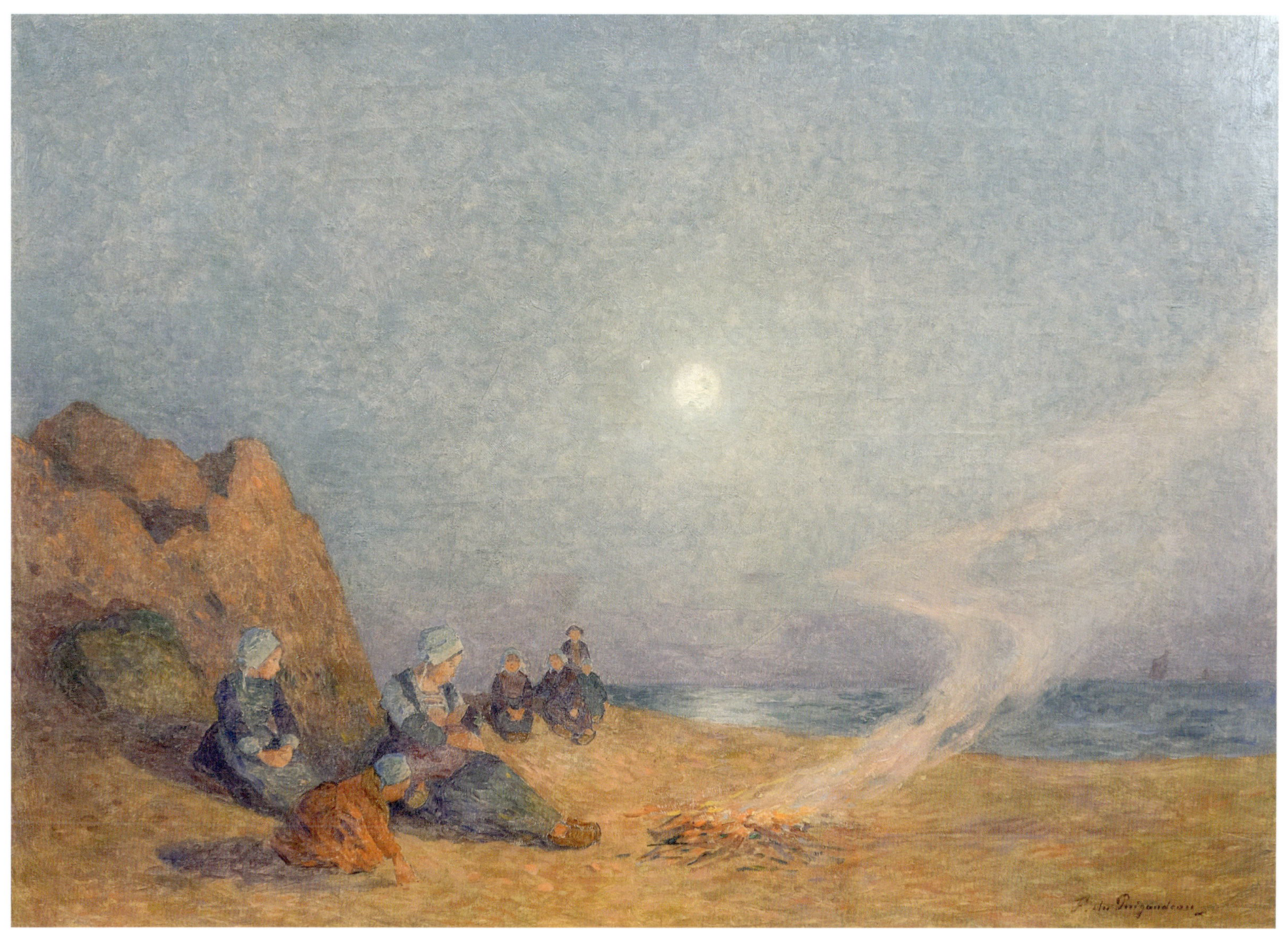

John Peter RUSSELL
(1858–1930)

Sunset over Morestil
Undated and unsigned
Oil on canvas
81 x 100 cm

John Peter Russell was of Scottish origin, although he was born in Darlinghurst, Australia. After the family engineering business was wound up, he left Sydney in 1882 to explore Europe. He attended art school in London before taking up an apprenticeship at the Cormon studio in Paris in 1885. While there he made the acquaintance of Anquetin, Bernard, Toulouse-Lautrec, and Van Gogh, among others. He loved the sea and travelled to Brittany in 1886 and again in 1888. In the end, he settled in Belle-Ile-en-Mer with his former model, lover, and wife Marianna Mattiocco, who also modelled for Rodin, building a house in the bay of Goulphar that included a large studio directly overlooking the ocean.

On his first trip to the small island of Morbihan in September 1886, Russell met the person he was to refer to as "the prince of Impressionists": Claude Monet. Following this momentous event in his life, Russell became the foremost Australian exponent of Impressionism. This work is a good example of his command of the technique, applying colour in short, urgent brushstrokes, often in juxtaposition, to match the motion of the waves crashing against the rocky coast, the frothing foam, and scudding clouds. His highly expressive style can be viewed as a harbinger of Fauvism.

Russell painted countless seascapes over the twenty-two years he spent on the island, anxious always to seize the changing moods of the same subject, painting at different times of the day, in all weathers and in different seasons. Unfortunately, most were neither signed nor dated, as if the artist was not content with the outcome.

When his wife died in 1908, the inconsolable Russell appears to have destroyed some 400 oil paintings and watercolours. This tragic event in his private life also led him to leave Belle-Ile. He returned to Australia in 1921 and died there in obscurity, before being rediscovered in 1978 when his work was the subject of a large international monographic exhibition held in his native country and the Netherlands.

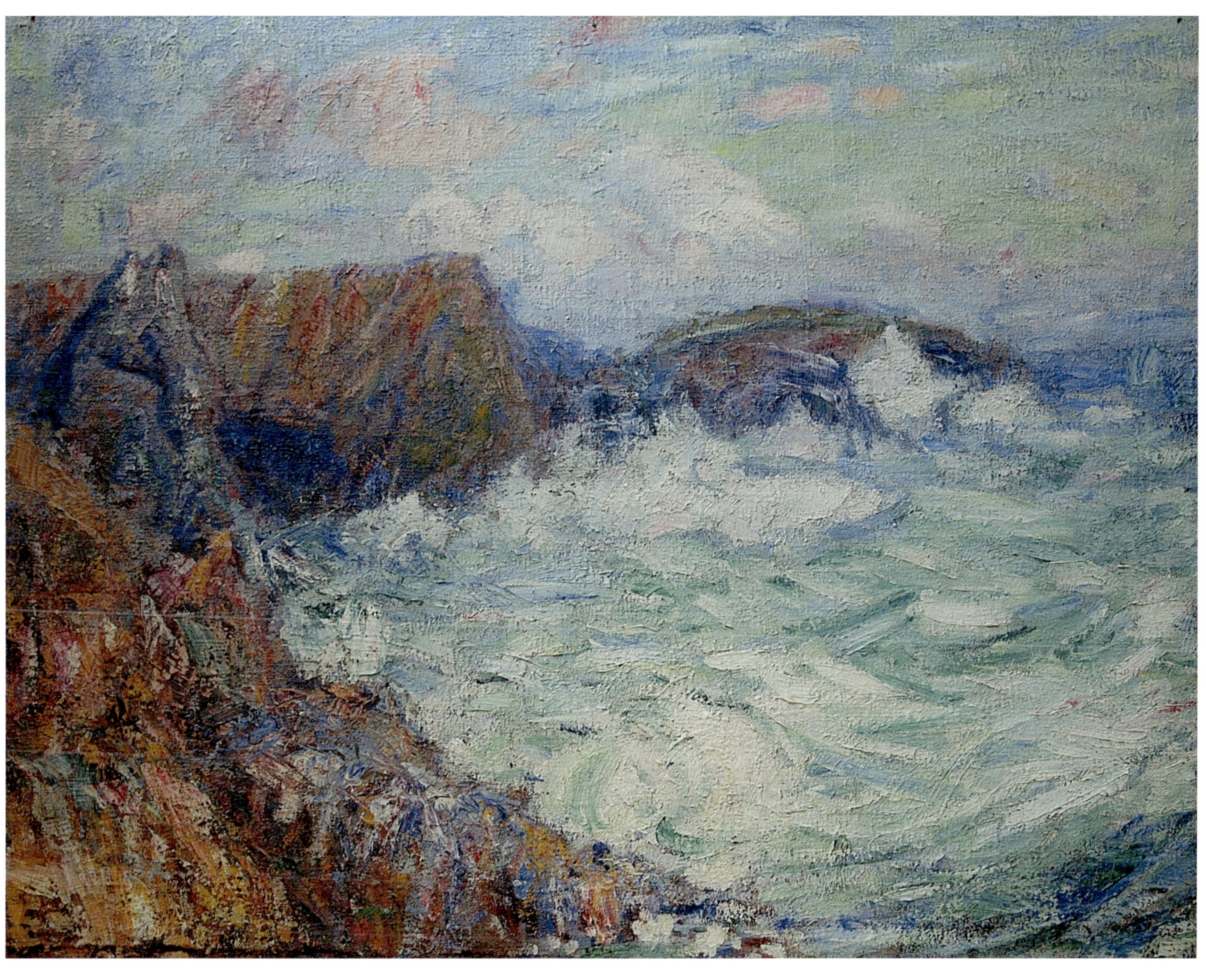

Armand SEGUIN (1869–1903)

Artificial Paradises, circa 1894–95
Unsigned
Oil on canvas
54 x 56 cm

While still training at the Académie Julian, Armand Seguin discovered the works of Paul Gauguin and Émile Bernard at the Café des Arts, right next to the brand new Eiffel Tower, in 1889. They were displayed in the famous Volpini exhibition along with other works by artists in the Impressionist and Synthetist group. In 1891, Seguin moved to Pont-Aven, where he made friends with the Irish artist Roderic O'Conor, who introduced him to etching. He took to it immediately and this was the technique he would increasingly turn to in his Breton works. Seguin's eclectic nature meant he enjoyed making synesthetic connections, so that from 1893 he also began to seek inspiration in literary sources.

As a lover of poetry, the artist has chosen in the present case to illustrate the verses of Baudelaire published in 1860 by Poulet-Malassis under the title *Artificial Paradises*. At the time drugs were thought to trigger a sort of transcendence and to induce sublime artistic visions. This almost square painting portrays the poet Paul Verlaine, on the right, experiencing what today would be called a "trip," during which he encounters a green monster, in the top left-hand corner, and a devil below playing a violin. The devil's facial features are undoubtedly those of Paul Gauguin. The apparitions include three female figures, the followers of Levana, the goddess of human dignity, who seem to be emerging from the flames.

Seguin stuck closely to the principles of Synthetism: in his works he uses clear outlines, pure colours applied in large fields, eliminating perspective. The pose of the woman with the raised arms seems to have been lifted directly from two of Gauguin's paintings: *In the Waves, Ondine I* (1889, Cleveland Museum of Art) and *Fatata te Miti by the Sea* (1892, National Gallery of Art, Washington, DC). The Japanese influence can be seen especially in the treatment of the crazed monster's pop eyes.

In around 1894, Seguin made another painting based on Baudelaire's most famous collection of poems *Les Fleurs du Mal*. But, although he nurtured an ambition to be a painter, prints continued to hold the greater attraction for him. Seguin contributed to *L'Occident,* the magazine founded by Adrien Mithouard and edited by Maurice Denis, right up to his death and was instrumental in gaining recognition for the Pont-Aven group, whose youngest member he was.

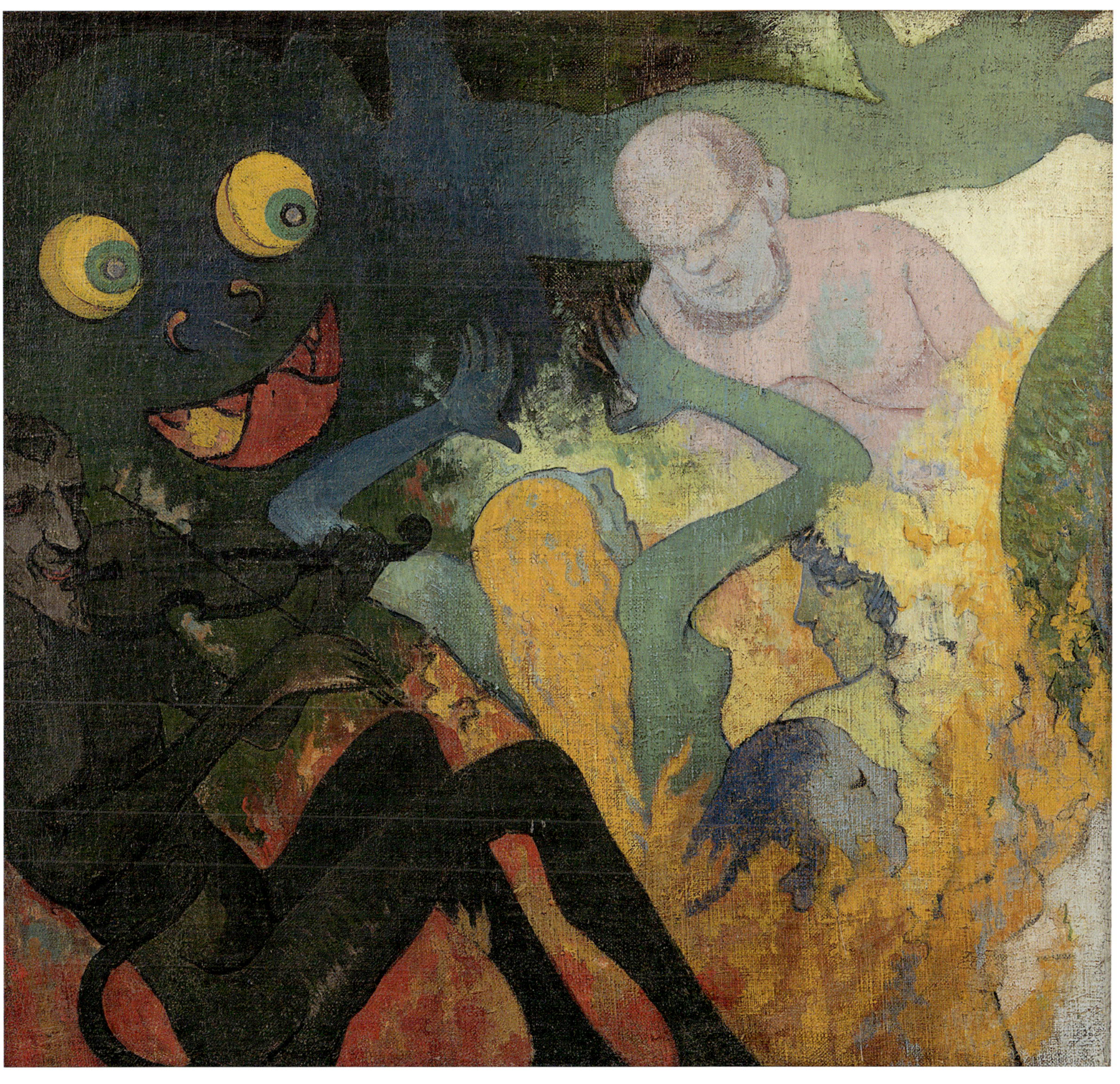

Armand SEGUIN (1869–1903)

Breton Woman (or *Nude with Hands behind her Head*), circa 1893–95
Unsigned
Etching and aquatint
16.2 x 6.2 cm

Armand Seguin entered the École des Arts Décoratifs in Paris in 1887, studying under Henri Ibels and Louis Roy. Attracted to Synthetism from his earliest studies, he decided in 1891 to spend in Pont-Aven as much time as he could. There he met Roderic O'Conor, who taught him the etching technique. Émile Bernard also said he worked with Seguin during the winter of 1892–93. This collaboration might have triggered Seguin's interest in Cloisonnism.

This etching is particularly original: the drawing is executed with finely etched, long strokes and looks as though it is carved in wood. Even the face resembles a wooden sculpture.

The delicacy of the lines building this figure and her headdress is truly exceptional. As a result, the artist is able to capture the sitter's melancholy mood with great subtlety. He renders the trees in the background with the swirling lines typical of his engravings of around 1893.

The work's vertical rectangular format, enhanced by the etched lines, recalls Japanese scroll prints. There is another very similar version of this print in a horizontal format that was published in *L'Ymagier* in April 1895.

The general public long remained unaware of Seguin's etchings, although he is undoubtedly one of the foremost engravers of the Pont-Aven group. This print too is in the Musée de Pont-Aven.

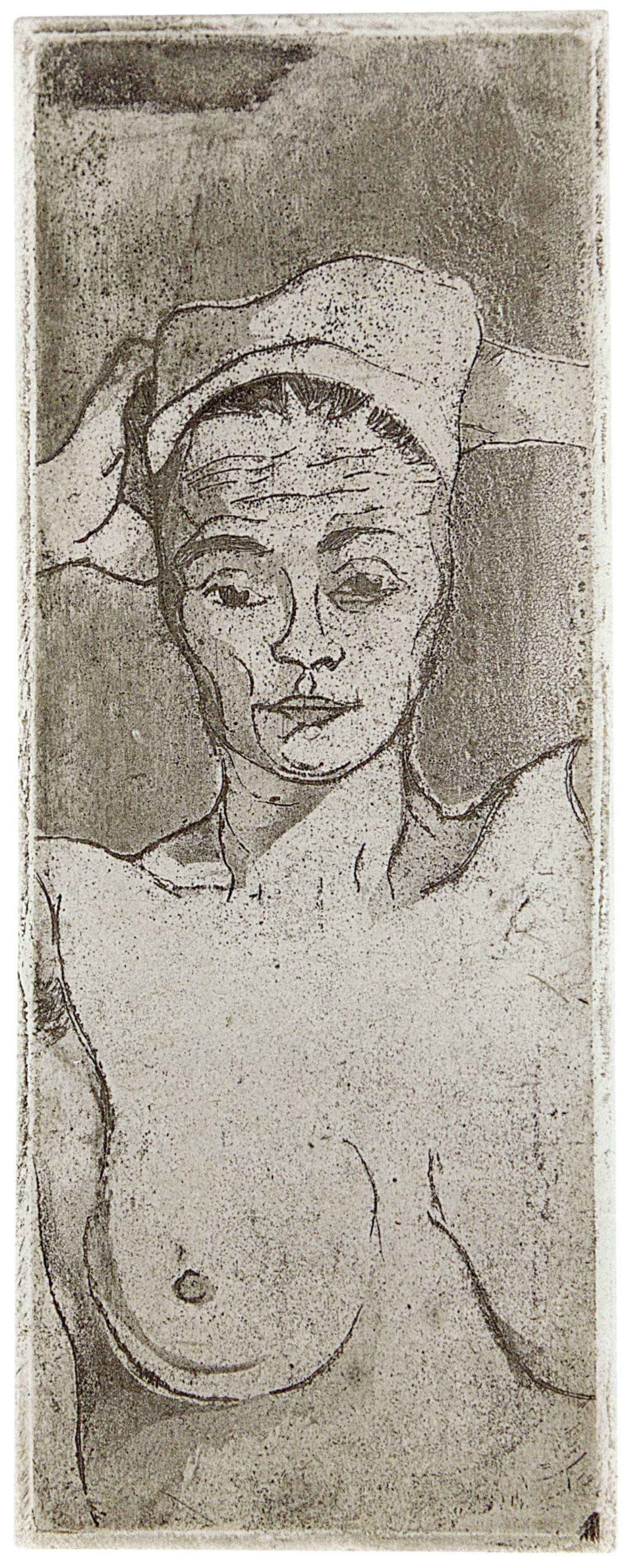

Paul SÉRUSIER (1864-1927)

The Fire Outside or *The Mammau,* or *Mammen*, 1893
Signed and dated on lower right
Oil on canvas
73 x 92 cm

This work's enigmatic title *The Mammau or Mammen* is said to mean "source of fresh water" in Breton, as well as "origin" or "mould," recalling a mother's role as a creator. Paul Sérusier was strongly drawn to the Huelgoat area in Finistère, finding there the setting for the transmission of legendary rituals that greatly fascinated him. Brittany played a key role in Sérusier's artistic development, the painter himself stating in 1893: "I feel more and more attracted to Brittany, which is my true home since that is where I was born in spirit."

In this work, he depicts several women wearing black headdresses by a lake. Some are preparing a meal, while others are making their way up the hill in a procession to join them. Apart from being a simple kitchen implement, the cauldron held by one of the women has a second meaning as a feature of pagan rituals. As such, it can be seen as symbolizing fire, magic spells, water, and even sometimes the female figure. In Celtic mythology, it is viewed as both the container of divine grace and as the source of artists' inspiration.

Sérusier accentuates the mystery by the skilful use of muted, flat colours whose unrealistic tones lend the scene a dreamlike mood, further highlighted by the golden light of sunset. As an exponent of Synthetism, he borrows from Gauguin his simple, undulating, and sometimes decorative line, as in the smoke spiralling up from the cauldron. He was also a great believer in matt colours, taking his cue from the distemper paintings of the Italian Primitives he so admired.

This work may be usefully compared with two other similar paintings by Sérusier: *The Incantation in the Sacred Wood* and *The Fern Harvesters,* where women are gathered together in a dark forest.

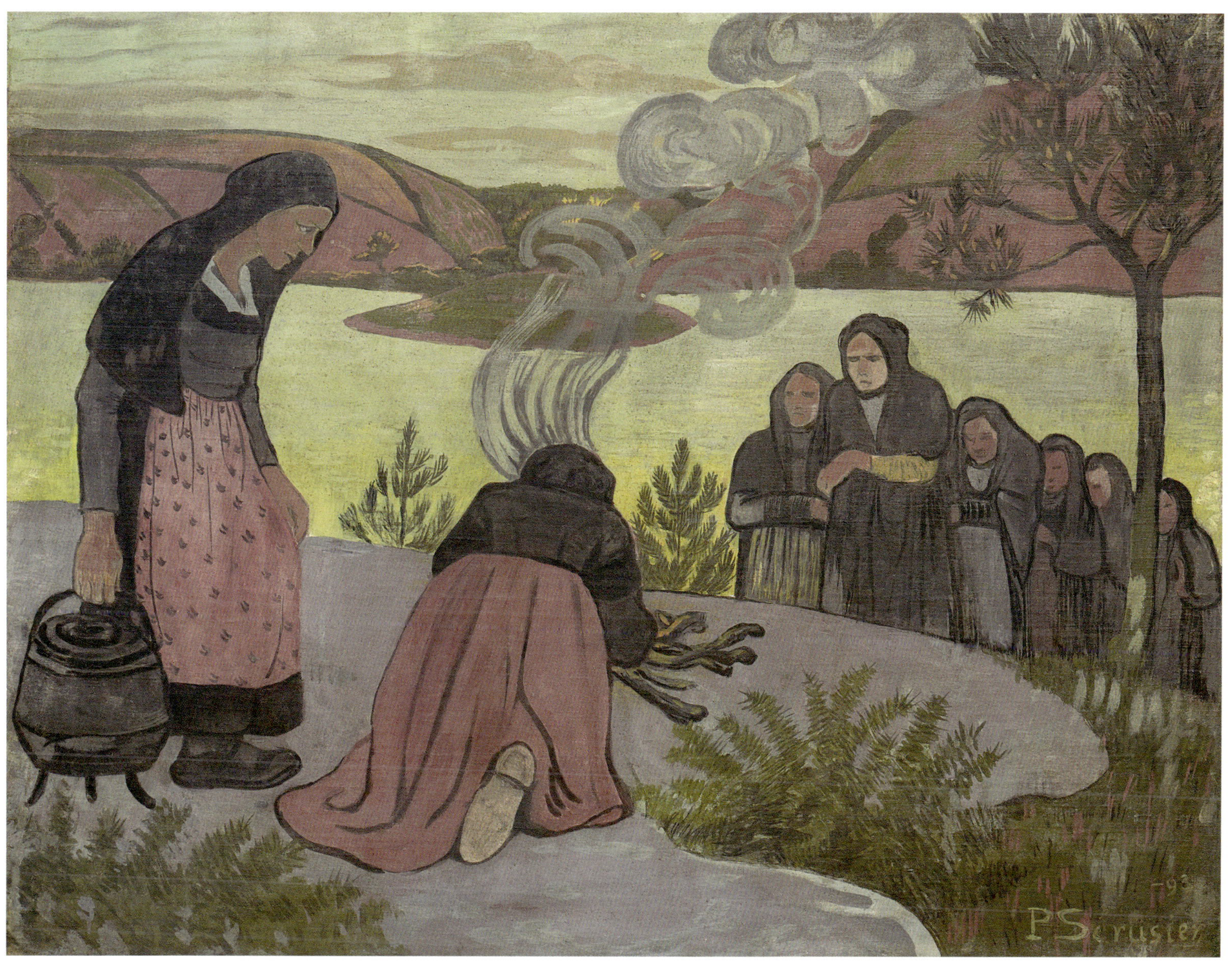
93
P. Sérusier

Paul SÉRUSIER (1864–1927)

Portrait of Émile Bernard in Florence, 1893
Initials "PS" on lower left
Tempera on canvas
73 x 56 cm

After flirting briefly with a career in business, Paul Sérusier attended the Académie Julian from 1886 to 1889. In the summer of 1888, he took his first trip to Pont-Aven and met Paul Gauguin. Under his supervision, Sérusier painted *The Talisman at the Bois d'Amour* (1888, Musée d'Orsay, Paris), which he took back to Paris to show his fellow artists, especially Pierre Bonnard, Maurice Denis, and Paul Ranson. The result was the blossoming of the Nabis group, prophets of a new, decorative form of art, in the wake of the Synthetism promoted by Gauguin and Bernard.

At Easter 1893, the "Nabi with the glistening beard" left Brittany for a few weeks and joined Émile Bernard in Florence. There he painted this portrait of the artist in all his youthful splendour. Sérusier shows him in half-length, seated on a terrace and gazing into the distance, with his hands folded daintily over an open book. His thick brown hair, loose dark grey jacket, blue waistcoat, and white shirt stand out against an emblematic background consisting of the Ponte Vecchio, the Duomo, and the surrounding hills. On the right can be seen an arcaded pavement in which two figures add extra depth of field to the painting, in the manner of Italian Renaissance artists.

The techniques of the so-called classic portrait have been adapted to suit a Synthetist purpose: spare, sinuous outlines, flat colour fields skilfully distributed around the canvas, and muted hues. In accordance with his theory of hot and warm colours, the painting can be divided into two clearly distinct sections: cold colours are reserved for the portrait itself, while warm colours are used in the landscape, which turns into a "decoration" designed to show off his friend to best advantage.

As was common among artists, Bernard also sketched a portrait of Sérusier.

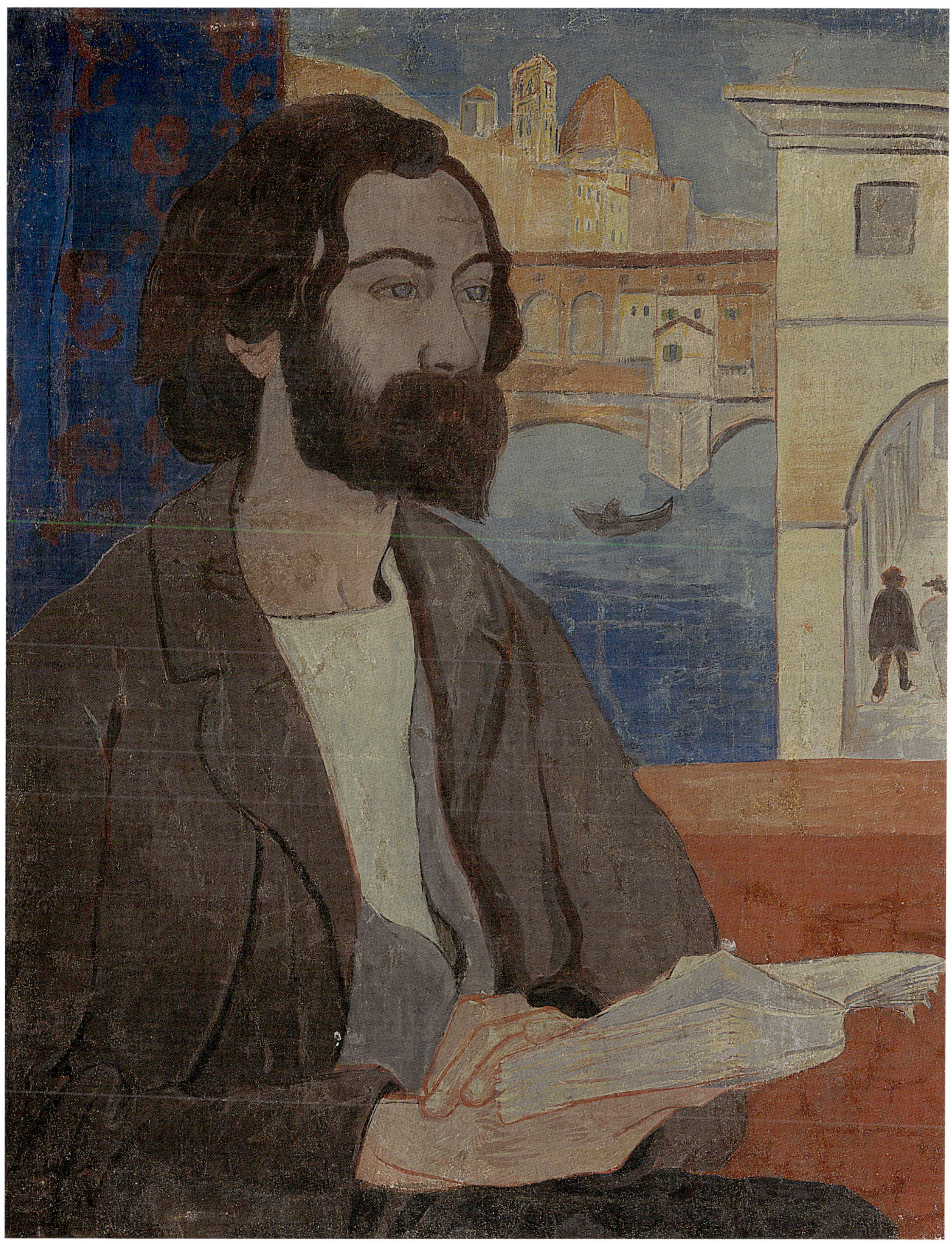

Paul SÉRUSIER (1864–1927)

The Red Wood, circa 1895
Signed on lower left
Oil on board mounted on canvas
120 x 60 cm

Forests were a very popular subject for paintings at the end of the nineteenth century. Whether in works of literature, such as Maeterlinck's *Pélléas et Mélisande,* or in painting, like Sérusier's *The Talisman* (1888), the "sacred grove" was viewed as a symbolic shelter for the restless soul.

In this example, the wooded landscape is suggested by metonymy, in the manner of the Japanese engravers, with a few tall, slender trees truncated at the top of the painting before reaching the canopy. The scattered granite boulders are perhaps based on the round rocks found at Huelgoat. Sérusier knew the area well, because after various trips to Pont-Aven and Le Pouldu, he finally settled in Huelgoat in 1892, before moving in 1906 to a house he adorned with wall paintings in Châteauneuf-du-Faou. In this work, he pares down his subject to the bare essential, making the effect all the more powerful by attaining a universal dimension.

As one of the guiding lights of the Nabis group, together with Maurice Denis and Edouard Vuillard, whom he met at the Lycée Condorcet in Paris, Paul Sérusier takes the principles Paul Gauguin taught him in Pont-Aven and employs them to stunning decorative effect in this painting. The work is characterised by its use of pure colours, chosen for their symbolic meaning rather than their representational validity. Red covers three-quarters of the painting's surface area, from the mossy ground to the surrounding vegetation, evoking autumn.

Included at number 1389 in the Salon des Indépendants, which ran from April 9 to May 26, 1895, this painting might date from the same year. It is certainly typical of Sérusier's work during this period, when the horizon and perspective all but disappear. To quote his friend Maurice Denis in his article titled "Définition du néotraditionnisme": "One must remember that before it depicts a warhorse, a nude or any other subject, a painting is essentially a flat surface covered with colours assembled in a certain order" (1890).

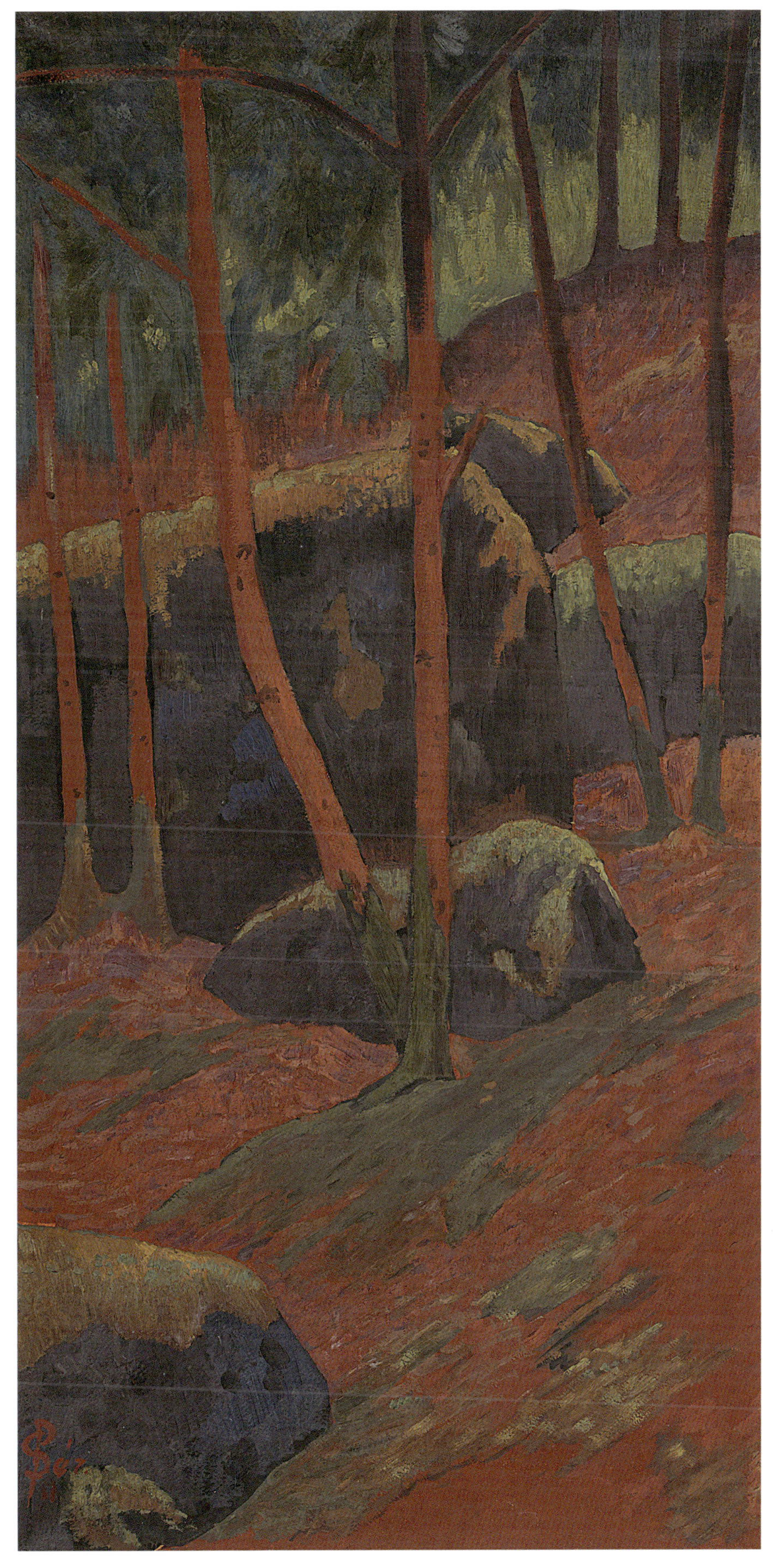

Władysław ŚLEWIŃSKI
(1856–1918)

Nature morte aux plats bleus
(Still Life with Blue Plates)
Undated and unsigned
Oil on canvas
74.5 x 92 cm

Władysław Ślewiński was a member of the Polish aristocracy and arrived in Paris in 1888. Unlike his compatriots, he did not receive any academic artistic training. Instead, he attended two private art schools, first the Académie Julian and then the Académie Colarossi, for around two years.

He probably met Paul Gauguin in 1889 in the restaurant Chez Madame Charlotte—a crucial encounter that encouraged him to persevere in his painting and planted in his mind the seeds of curiosity about Brittany. The exhibition of works by the Impressionist and Synthetist group held at the Café Volpini that same year also made a great impression on him.

Contrary to the established hierarchy of genres, Ślewiński loved painting flowers, and indeed it was as a sitter competing for attention with a stunning bouquet of flowers that Gauguin chose to portray him (National Museum of Western Art, Tokyo). Rejecting figurative accuracy, Ślewiński here depicts the flowers as blotches of red paint against an indistinct background. The flowers have been placed in a Delft vase among other blue vases of the same kind arranged on a tablecloth with an orange ground and a complementary blue pattern.

In one of his "Lettres de Paris" he wrote for the review *Wiesy*, the Russian poet and artist Maximilian Volochine states: " . . . in Ślewiński's still lifes, each of his objects speaks in a mysterious, musical tone like an evening chant quavering like the nostalgia that one's native land awakes. The painter possesses this gift, thanks to which everything he touches echoes with a melancholy moan . . . The painter's favourite colours are dark violet and pale blue, reflecting mystical and mysterious moods" (in the exhibition catalogue of *Władysław Ślewiński, 1854-1918,* Musée de Pont-Aven, 1981, p. 14).

According to the Polish art historian Władysława Jaworska, the still lifes are among the artist's most personal works, in which he made his most daring experiments, as he does here.

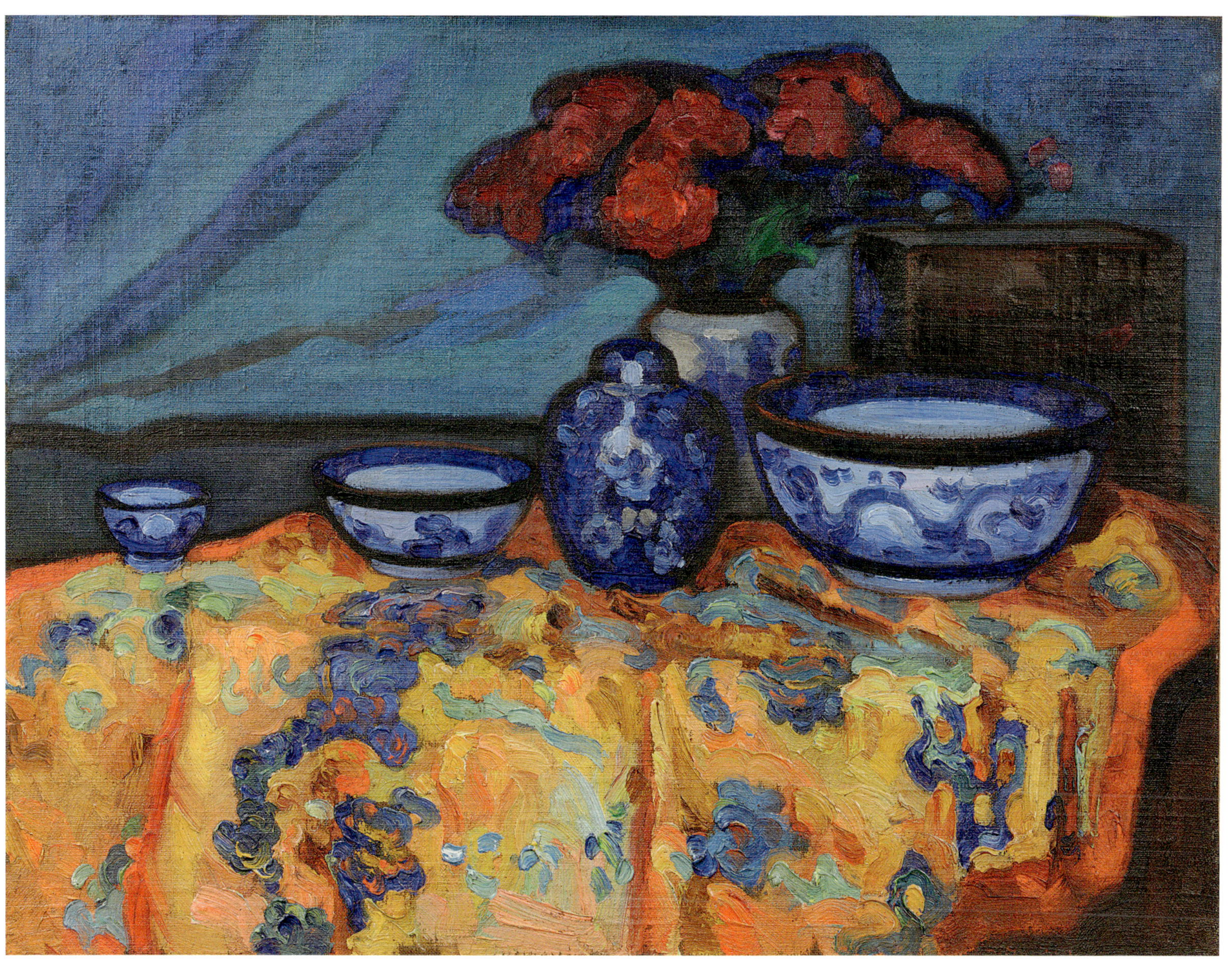

Władysław ŚLEWIŃSKI
(1856–1918) attributed

Presumed Portrait of Henryk Sienkiewicz, Author of Quo Vadis? (recto)
Undated and unsigned
Oil on canvas
92 x 65 cm

Landscape with Bridge (verso)

The works Ślewiński saw in the 1889 exhibition in the so-called Café Volpini made a deep impression on him. Captivated by the novel concepts of Gauguin and his circle, he decided to abandon his academic training and join them.

There are two theories regarding the sitter's identity: the portrait either depicts an architect with his mock-up or Henryk Sienkiewicz (1846–1916), one of the greatest Polish authors of the nineteenth century, at his writing desk. Sienkiewicz wrote historical novels and earned lasting fame, and the 1905 Nobel Prize for literature, when *Quo Vadis?,* set in Nero's Rome, was published in 1896. While the figure itself is very simply handled, the face, shown in three-quarter view, is much more clearly detailed. The artist uses the angle of the light and the flat, almost Fauve colours to bring out the eyes and cheeks and to give weight to the hands resting on the desk.

Ślewiński here displays a full adherence to the artistic technique adopted by the Pont-Aven group: form is radically simplified, features are deliberately truncated, and colours are applied in large fields and enclosed by clearly defined outlines. The artist concentrates on conveying his subject's personality. The crimson background further helps to underline the sitter's romantic aspects.

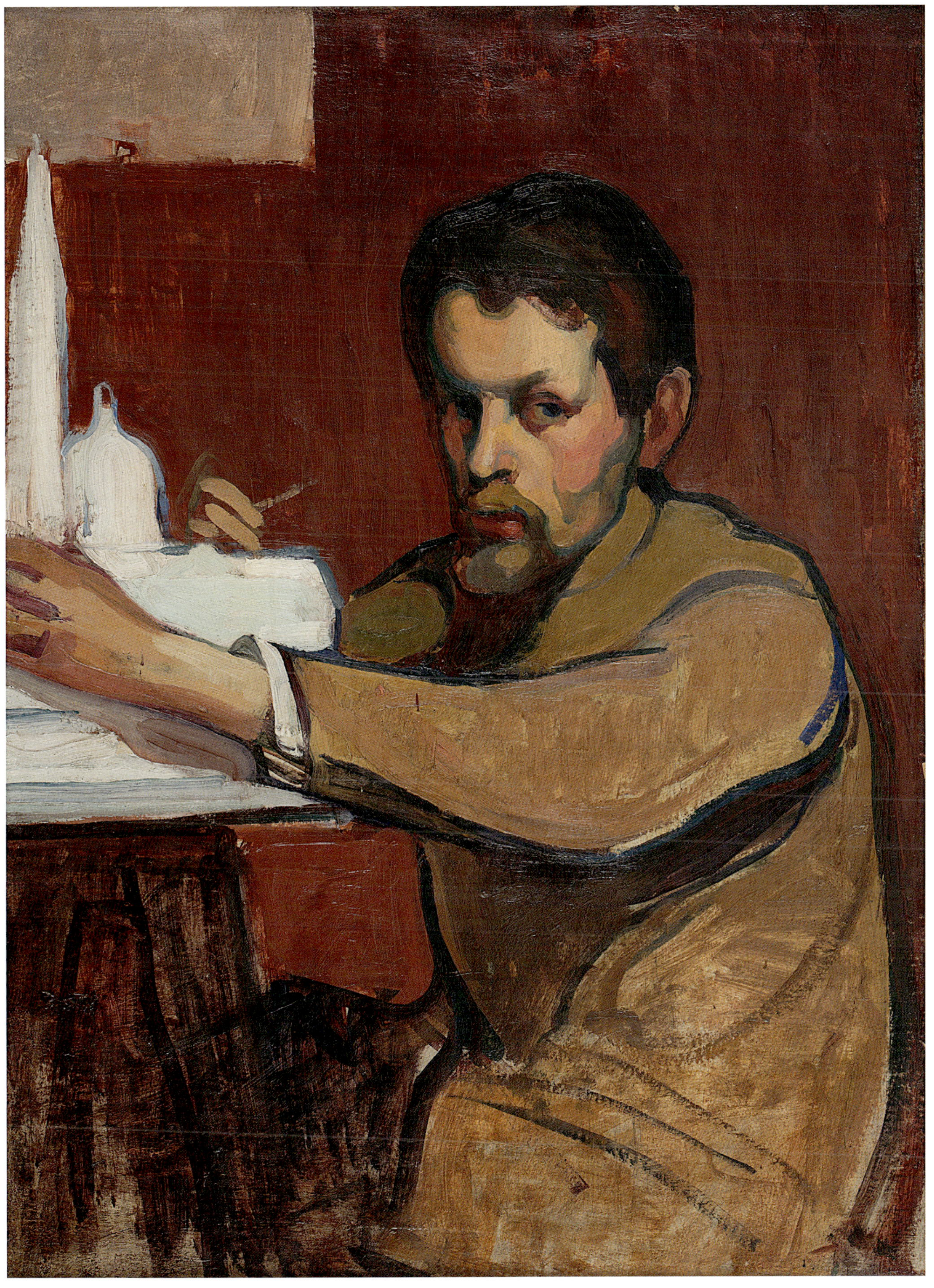

Jan VERKADE (1868–1946)

Landscape with Haystacks, 1891
Signed and dated on lower left
Oil on canvas
53 x 64 cm

Jan Verkade was the son of a Dutch biscuit maker. He joined the Nabis group when he moved to Paris in 1891. Like all the other members of the group, he as well had a nickname, *nabi obéliscal* [the obelisk-like Nabi], on account of being very tall. Taking Meijer de Haan's advice, he decided in April of that same year to walk to Brittany in the wake of Paul Gauguin and in the company of the Danish artist Mogens Ballin. Verkade was taken by the countryside, with its orderly farms, winding paths, and gentle hills. He settled for a time in Le Pouldu, near Pont-Aven, where he began painting *en plein air*, as testified by *Landscape with Haystacks*.

He stayed in Brittany only twelve months and this period in his life is represented by very few surviving paintings, such as this one. Synthetism's influence is immediately apparent: like Émile Bernard in *Yellow Tree*, he treats the haystacks and trees extremely schematically, as round forms emerging from the surrounding space. He chooses bright, sometimes reddish colours, underlining that this is an autumnal scene. Verkade is thought to have left Brittany in around mid-October 1891, making his way back to Holland.

Jan Verkade's spiritual journey led him to convert to Roman Catholicism, taking holy orders in 1902. He died in the Archabbey of Beuron in Germany. His autobiography, *Die Unrue zu Gott*, published in English in 1930 as *Yesterdays of an Artist-Monk*, traces his spiritual development.

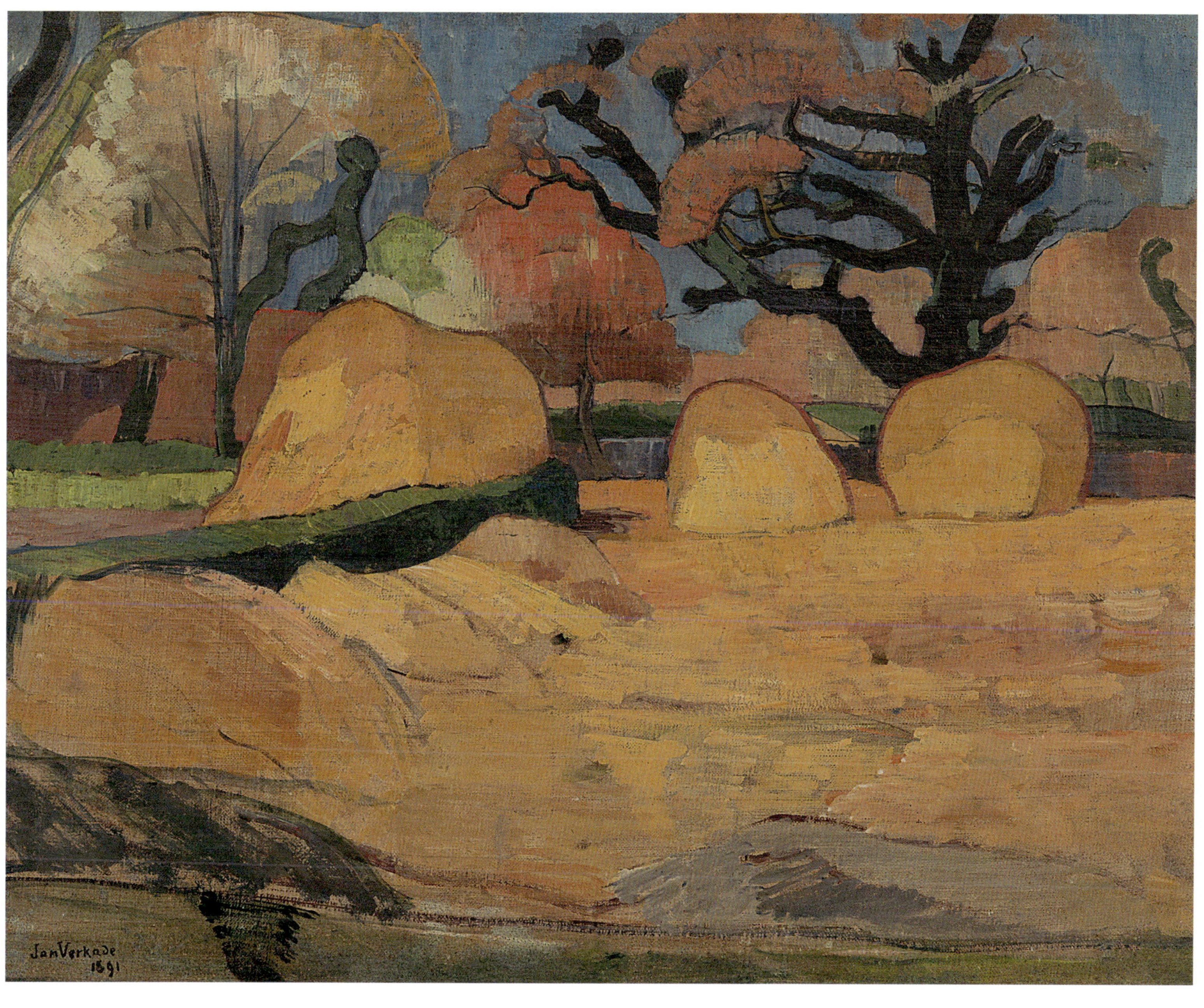
Jan Verkade
1891

BIBLIOGRAPHY

Principal Works and Articles in Order of Publication

1971 Władysława Jaworska. *Gauguin. L'école de Pont-Aven.* Neuchâtel: Éditions Ides et Calendes.

1986 Władysława Jaworska and Catherine Puget. *1886-1986. Cent ans Gauguin à Pont-Aven* (exhibition catalogue), Pont-Aven, Musée de Pont-Aven (June 28 – September 30, 1986).

1987 Denise Delouche and Catherine Puget. *Émile Jourdan (1860-1931)* (exhibition catalogue), Pont-Aven, Musée de Pont-Aven (June 27 – September 30, 1987).

1988 Caroline Godfroy Durand-Ruel, Catherine Puget, and Claire Sauvage. *Henry Moret, aquarelles et peintures (1856-1913)* (exhibition catalogue), Pont-Aven, Musée de Pont-Aven (June 26 – September 26, 1988).

1989 Jos Pennec and Catherine Puget. *Armand Seguin (1869-1903)* (exhibition catalogue), Pont-Aven, Musée de Pont-Aven (June 25 – October 10, 1989).

1991 Caroline Boyle-Turner and Catherine Puget. *Paul Sérusier et la Bretagne* (exhibition catalogue), Pont-Aven, Musée de Pont-Aven (June 30 – September 30, 1991).

1993 Antoine Terrasse. *Pont-Aven l'école buissonnière*. Paris: Éditions Gallimard, series "Découvertes."

1994 Caroline Boyle-Turner and Catherine Puget. *Le Cercle de Gauguin en Bretagne* (exhibition catalogue), Pont-Aven, Musée de Pont-Aven (June 25 – September 26, 1994).

André Cariou. *Les Peintres de Pont-Aven.* Rennes: Éditions Ouest-France.

1996 Roger Le Brun. *Marie-Jeanne Gloanec (1839-1915).* Pont-Aven: Association des Amis du Musée de Pont-Aven.

1997 Richard Brettell, Denise Delouche, and Catherine Puget. *Gauguin et l'école de Pont-Aven* (exhibition catalogue), Pont-Aven, Musée de Pont-Aven (June 28 – September 29, 1997).

1998 Fernande Rivet-Daoudal. *Pont-Aven. Impressions de voyageurs (1856-1910).* Pont-Aven: Association des Amis du Musée de Pont-Aven.

1999 Julian Campbell and Catherine Puget. *Peintres irlandais en Bretagne (1870-1930)* (exhibition catalogue), Pont-Aven, Musée de Pont-Aven (June 26 – September 27, 1999).

2000 Isabelle Cahn and Catherine Puget. *Gauguin et le Christ jaune* (exhibition catalogue), Pont-Aven, Musée de Pont-Aven (June 24 – October 2, 2000).

2002 Fernande Rivet-Daoudal. *Mademoiselle Julia (1848-1927).* Pont-Aven: Association des Amis du Musée de Pont-Aven.

2003 Denise Delouche and Catherine Puget. *Kenavo Monsieur Gauguin* (exhibition catalogue), Pont-Aven, Musée de Pont-Aven (June 28 - September 29, 2003).

2004 Julian Campbell and Catherine Puget. *Peintres britanniques en Bretagne* (exhibition catalogue), Pont-Aven, Musée de Pont-Aven (June 26 - September 27, 2004).

2006 Daniel Morane and Catherine Puget. *L'Estampe en Bretagne (1880-1960)* (exhibition catalogue), Pont-Aven, Musée de Pont-Aven (March 18 - June 19, 2006).

Jacqueline Duroc and Léo Kerlo. *Peintres des côtes de Bretagne*. Douarnenez: Éditions du Chasse-marée, vol. IV.

Philippe Bonnet, Denise Delouche, and Catherine Puget. *Peintres de la Bretagne et quête spirituelle* (exhibition catalogue), Pont-Aven, Musée de Pont-Aven (June 24 - September 25, 2006).

Belinda Thomson. *La Vision de Gauguin*. Quimper: Éditions Palantines.

Estelle Fresneau. "Le musée des Beaux-Arts de Pont-Aven," *Dossier de l'art*, no. 135. Dijon, pp. 82–85.

2007 Denise Delouche and Estelle Fresneau. *Pont-Aven, du paysage à l'œuvre* (exhibition catalogue), Pont-Aven, Musée de Pont-Aven (June 30 - October 1, 2007).

2008 Estelle Guille des Buttes-Fresneau. *Pont-Aven et ses peintres*. Luçon: Éditions Jean-Paul Gisserot, series "Patrimoine culturel."

2009 Denise Delouche and Estelle Guille des Buttes-Fresneau. *Maurice Denis (1870-1943) et la Bretagne - La leçon de Pont-Aven* (exhibition catalogue), Pont-Aven, Musée de Pont-Aven (June 6 - October 5, 2009), Quimper: Éditions Palantines.

Meijer de Haan, le maître caché (exhibition catalogue), Amsterdam, Jewish Museum (13 October 2009 - 24 January 2010) / Paris, Musée d'Orsay (16 March - 20 June 2010) / Quimper, Musée des Beaux-Arts, 9 July - 11 October 2010). Paris: Editions Hazan.

2010 Estelle Guille des Buttes-Fresneau (ed.). *Pont-Aven, un musée, une collection*. Paris: Éditions Somogy.

2011 Denise Delouche. *Les Peintres de la Bretagne*. Quimper: Éditions Palantines.

2013 *Les peintres de Pont-Aven autour de Gauguin 1886-1920* (exhibition catalogue), Ville de Rueil Malmaison, Atelier Grognard (12 January - 8 April 2013). Colombelles: Editions du Valhermeil.

2015 André Cariou. *Gauguin et l'école de Pont-Aven*. Paris: Éditions Hazan.

2017 David Haziot. *Gauguin*. Paris: Fayard.

CONTRIBUTORS' BIOGRAPHIES

Estelle Guille des Buttes obtained her diploma from the École du Louvre and Institut National du Patrimoine in Paris and is Chief Curator of the Musée de Pont-Aven, which she has run since 2006, overseeing its extension and restoration. She has organized several exhibitions, including *Maurice Denis et la Bretagne* in 2009, earmarked by the Ministry of Culture as being of national interest, and in 2017 *La Modernité en Bretagne (1870-1940)*. Estelle Guille des Buttes is also the author of numerous articles and other publications on the Pont-Aven School. She has been granted the title of Chevalier des Arts et Lettres.

Adrien Goetz is a member of the Institute (Academy of Fine Arts), a former student of the École Normale Supérieure, and holds an agrégation in History and a PhD in the History of Art. At present, he teaches the History of Art at the University of Paris-Sorbonne. He has a special interest in the art of the nineteenth century. Adrien Goetz also writes novels, which are set in an art world or museum context. He is Chief Editor of *Grande Galerie. Le Journal du Louvre*, the museum's official magazine. He writes a column for *Le Figaro* every Monday titled "Les Arts."

Jean-Marie Rouart was born at Neuilly-sur-Seine on April 8, 1943 into a family of painters. He is a writer and journalist and published his first novel *La Fuite en Pologne* in 1974. His novel *Avant-guerre* won the Prix Renaudot in 1983. His other novels include *Le Cavalier blessé*, 1987; *La Femme de proie*, 1989; *Le Voleur de jeunesse*, 1990; *Le Goût du malheur*, 1993; *L'Invention de l'amour*, 1997. In addition to writing novels and essays, Jean-Marie Rouart has also pursued a parallel career in journalism, firstly at *Magazine littéraire*, then at *Le Figaro* and *Quotidien de Paris*, where he edited the literary section. Following his period as editor of *Figaro littéraire*, from 1986 to 2003, he started writing for *Paris Match*. He was elected to the French Academy on December 18, 1997.

PHOTO CREDITS

Page 13: © 2017 White Images/Scala, Firenze
Page 16: © 2017 Foto Scala, Firenze
Page 18: © 2017 Image copyright The Metropolitan Museum of Art/Art Resource/ Scala, Firenze
Page 23: © Thierry-Lannon et Associés
Page 25: © Bernard Galeron
Page 27: © Bernard Galeron
Page 29: © P-Y Dhinaut
Page 31: © P-Y Dhinaut
Page 33: © Didier Robcis
Page 35: © All rights reserved
Page 37: © Didier Robcis
Page 39: © Didier Robcis
Page 41: © All rights reserved
Page 43: © P-Y Dhinaut
Page 45: © P-Y Dhinaut
Page 47: © Didier Robcis
Page 49: © Didier Robcis
Page 51: © Didier Robcis
Page 53: © Thierry Lannon & Associés
Page 55: © All rights reserved
Page 57: © Didier Robcis
Page 59: © Guillaume de Roquemaurel
Page 61: © Bernard Galeron
Page 63: © Didier Robcis
Page 65: © Didier Robcis
Page 67: © P-Y Dhinaut
Page 69: © Didier Robcis
Page 71: © Didier Robcis